THE RATIONALITY OF FAITH

By CARL MICHALSON

The Rationality of Faith
The Witness of Kierkegaard
Japanese Contributions to Christian Theology
The Hinge of History
Faith for Personal Crises
Christianity and the Existentialists, Editor

CARL MICHALSON

THE RATIONALITY OF FAITH

An Historical Critique of the Theological Reason

SCM PRESS LTD
BLOOMSBURY STREET LONDON

First British edition 1964

Printed in the United States of America

To my brother and sisters

Gordon

Edna

Eva

ἡγιασμένοις

PREFACE

THIS volume was precipitated by an invitation to give the James W. Richard lectures in the Christian Religion at the University of Virginia in the fall of 1961. A Faculty Fellowship from the American Association of Theological Schools combined with a sabbatical leave from Drew University made possible a year of study in Strasbourg, France, during which the lectures were composed.

A doctrinal revolution is occurring in our time. New understandings of history, language, and the science of interpretation called hermeneutics are the main factors inspiring it. Traditional theological methods of reflection upon faith have been derived from philosophies whose apparent validities have lately eroded. New understandings of the structure of reality are providing opportunities for more meaningful access to the reality of faith. The tendency has been simply to paste these new understandings to the old formulations. That has been helpful and illuminating and has paved the way for more thorough reflection on the nature of Christian faith. In these lectures, however, I have attempted to regularize and carry forward the suggestions for more radical revision of theological method which my book, *The Hinge of History*, has proposed.

As usual my debt to others ranges far beyond the acknowledgments carried in the footnotes. A few of the more obvious should be mentioned. Working in Strasbourg while I was there were Professors George Williams of Harvard University, Gibson Winter of the University of Chicago, and L. E. Shiner of Cornell College.

Each read this work in its preliminary form and from their various perspectives I received valuable suggestions for its improvement. Mrs. Polly Leidenberg typed the first draft and Mrs. Pat Winters typed the final draft and helped with the proofs and indexing.

The substance of the volume was also used for the Kearns Lectures in the Duke University Graduate School's department of religion. The small sections on language scattered throughout chapters two and three were drawn together as an editorial entitled "Language, History and Meaning" for *Theology Today,* April, 1962.

The problem I have chosen to examine here is methodological and therefore at the base of all theological reflection. That I was limited to three lectures was benevolent, for systematic thinking depends not so much upon demonstration of point after point as upon the coherence and illumination of the case as a whole. The beginning and the end should be seen together. This is patently easier to achieve in a series limited to three lectures than in a *summa theologica* or under the relatively interminable conditions of an academic year.

I am especially grateful to have been forced to think through these matters in the presence of an academic community the edge of whose critique need never be blunted by the learned caution of more ecclesiastical communities. In matters of history, nothing should be held in secret. At the same time, I trust that in attempting to make myself understood to this particular kind of audience I will not become so exotic to my fellow-theologians that, like Daniel Defoe, I will be pilloried by my own party.

Carl Michalson

Drew Forest
Madison, N. J.

CONTENTS

THE RATIONALITY OF FAITH

INTRODUCTION

History is the best and only philosophy.

JOHANN GEORG HAMANN, Letter to Jacobi,
April 25, 1786.

History is 'human'; nothing human is alien to it, not even the Christian faith.

GERHARD KRÜGER, *Freiheit und Verwaltung*,
Freiburg and Munich, 1958, p. 159.

THE Christian faith is an attitude toward the world which the presence of Jesus of Nazareth in history has made possible. Attachment to this event makes Christianity unique, in the sense that any conviction is unique if attached to some pivotal event. One has one's attitude toward the world through the mediation of particular historical events. Being tied to history in this way sets Christian understanding within the framework of historical methods in general and thus in contradistinction to non-historical methods, such as those which the natural and metaphysical sciences inspire.

Vacillation between historical and non-historical methods is a major source of confusion in the modern world over whether the Christian faith is reasonable. I say "in the modern world" because history as a deliberate method of understanding distinct from other methods is a relatively modern enterprise. The Christian faith is historically based, therefore the methods of thinking in a Christian's faith are destined to be historical. Yet, up to this moment in the theology of the church, Christians have not profited fully enough from the methods of reflection available in this modern phenomenon. More than anything intrinsic to Christianity itself, failure to think the faith historically accounts for confusions and disagreements among theologians, private Christians and the people of the world. They cannot agree as to whether reason and faith are harmonious, paradoxical, or contradictory. Such problems regarding the rationality of faith could seem somewhat professional and abstract were it not that their solution promises to admit the Christian to a more authentic appreciation of his faith and to give contemporary culture a more sporting chance to be illumined by this faith.

My goal, therefore, will be to describe the rationality of the Christian faith. Rationality is a contextual concept. Inasmuch as the context of the Christian faith is history, I will specify its rationality by setting the Christian faith in the context of history alone. In pursuing this goal I will necessarily be guided by a great variety of intellectual suggestions. Most refreshing of all to me as theologian is the realization that for probably the first time in the history of the church the formulations of theology must now be instructed by the historiographers more than by the philosophers. The virgin thrill of this discovery is soon compromised, however. From the side of the working historians a theologian gets little encouragement when he sees that they themselves benefit very little from the choicest insights of their own methodologists. Historians continue to write what Paul Valéry called "historians' history," one perilous step removed from the world men live. That is why, when I speak of history, I will mean approximately what Wilhelm Dilthey meant when he said, "History is at every point life. And history consists of life of every sort in the most different relations. History is but life comprehended from the viewpoint of the whole of humanity."[1]

From the side of the professional theologians the encouragement in the use of this kind of lived history is no greater. No major theologian today fails to announce on almost every page of his work that the Christian revelation, from which all theological insight emanates, is historical. At the same time, not even the greatest among these system builders has put history at the center, allowing it to structure his system. Theology is still being delineated today as if before the rise of the historical consciousness. In these pages, however, it is my intention to think as theologian exclusively within the framework of history. I am persuaded that it is possible to say of theology what Benedetto Croce said of his philosophy: it is the method of historiography.

Notwithstanding this primacy of history as a discipline, philosophy continues to be an indispensable dialogical partner of theology, especially the philosophies which are sensitive to the reality of history. Among these one cannot classify naturalisms and materialisms, although one might profitably include dialectical mate-

[1] *Gesammelte Schriften*, Leipzig and Berlin, 1921ff., Vol. VII, p. 256.

rialisms. Nor can one classify idealisms, although the idealists from Kant to Hegel were the first philosophers to be scholars in the sense in which historians are scholars, and the first therefore to introduce the structures of history into the concepts of philosophy.

There are three current philosophies, however, which have become singularly efficient in exercising midwifery upon the body of the Christian faith. One is known as logical analysis. That this philosophy should be useful to historical methods emerges as a minor miracle, considering that in its origin it deliberately bound itself to the physical sciences. The current emphasis among the Oxford analysts on the methodological confusion which results from the mixing of categories is now of cardinal importance in facilitating the detection of ambiguities which develop when the word "history" is employed. The most basic step in clarifying the question of how to think about an historical faith is to determine in what senses it can be said that Christianity is historical, and to keep these senses cleanly differentiated.[2]

Another philosophy integral to the definition of history is phenomenology. This philosophy has formulated, more clearly than any other to my knowledge, what it is that differentiates approaches to history from approaches to nature, why it is that these

[2] A beginning was made in this direction in my book, *The Hinge of History*, An Existential Approach to the Christian Faith, Scribners, 1959. There I employed an analogy to dimensions which I learned from Karl Heim, although Heim did not use it with respect to historical reality. The analogy has the advantage of showing how a single reality like history can have a multiple structure and how the singleness of the reality does not excuse one from distinguishing between its various dimensions. Since employing this expression I have found it everywhere I look, although never rigorously applied. See especially Raymond Aron, *Dimensions de la conscience historique*, Paris, 1961. Also, Maurice Merleau-Ponty, *Phénoménologie de la Perception*, Paris, 1945, p. xiii:

> In each civilization it is a matter of rediscovering the idea in the Hegelian sense, that is to say, not as a law of the physico-mathematical type, accessible to objective thought, but the model of a unique behavior toward others, toward Nature, toward time and toward death, a certain

two approaches are radically immiscible, and how a realization of that distinction affects the very structure of reason. Where this philosophy is known it has acquired a bad reputation, chiefly for two characteristics. It is conceptually obscure and it is preoccupied with "ideas" to the neglect of the evident stuff of existence. To guard against this drift in my own philosophical contacts, I have fastened myself to those phenomenologists most influenced by the late, more historical writings of phenomenology's founder, Edmund Husserl. I refer above all to Jean-Paul Sartre and the late Maurice Merleau-Ponty. These two philosophers have two additional virtues. They are French, which means, as Ludwig Feuerbach long ago pointed out, they can be counted on for clarity. They are also Marxist in orientation, which means their phenomenology embraces a highly materialized form of history. Yet, because this philosophy is phenomenology, its materialism is not the materialism of nature but of history. That distinction, already implicit in the Christian faith, is utterly imperative for an understanding of how a man of faith reasons historically.

The third philosophy is the contemporary movement most passionately historical in its orientation, that is, existentialism. Just by its strategy of immersion in life, this philosophy has done more than any other non-religious point of view to articulate the

---

manner of shaping the world that the historian ought to be able to estimate and employ. These are the *dimensions* (italics his) of history. In my discussion of the dimensions I specified four: world history, existential history, Biblical history, and eschatological history. I would want to relate these dimensions, in terms of a phrase Merleau-Ponty uses elsewhere with a slightly different bearing, as "sectors of experience irreducible to each other." (*La Structure du Comportement*, Paris, 1942; third edition, 1953, p. 186.) The Japanese philosopher, Kiyoshi Miki, also worked with four "dimensions" of history called being, logos, the sources, and the actuality, dialectically related, hence not mutually exclusive. (*Rekishi-Tetsugaku* [The Philosophy of History], Tokyo, 1947, pp. 100-138. See the discussion of his distinctions in my *Japanese Contributions to Christian Theology*, Westminster Press, 1960, pp. 159ff.) The Spanish philosopher, Ortega y Gasset, finds "three great

structures and limits of history. In its dialogue with theology, therefore, it has served both to purify the Christian faith of untenable excesses and to instruct the faith in the precise character of its rapport with the world.

Finally, however, I must confess that I am vocationally neither an historian nor a philosopher. I am a "theologian." That means I am responsible for saying what it means to be a Christian and how that meaning affects man's other attitudes toward the world. That stance may even seem culturally menacing when it is realized that the Christian faith is an eschatological reality which sets all life within the framework of an ultimate claim.

When I sub-titled *The Hinge of History* "An Existential Approach to the Christian Faith," I did not expect the book to be described as "an existential theology." Existentialism is an approach to the Christian faith in the same sense in which a porch is an approach to a house. The Christian does not live on the porch and the existentialist does not enter the house without ceasing to be an existentialist. There seems to be a widespread conviction in theology today that the title "existential theology" is a tautology. I would call it a contradiction. Existentialism is the expression of the fundamental meaninglessness of existence. The Christian faith is just the opposite, the revelation of fundamental meaning.

Possibly on that basis, the adoption of history as the model for theological thinking should be looked upon as a bit intrusive, if not absurd. Possibly in history there are no ultimates, or ought not to

---

vital dimensions" of historical activity "essentially hostile to each other." Knowledge of these dimensions is said to expose "the error which is hidden in the apparent clarity of a date." (*What is Philosophy?*, tr. by Mildred Adams, W. W. Norton & Co., 1960, pp. 33ff.) Probably the discovery most disarming to me has been the work of the sixteenth-century French historian, Jean Bodin, who developed "four kinds of history," human, natural, mathematical and sacred. (*La Methode de l'Histoire*, 1572, translation from the Latin by Pierre Mesnard, Paris, 1941. In English as John Bodin, *Method for the Easy Comprehension of History*, translated by Beatrice Reynolds, Columbia University Press, 1945; see especially pp. 15-19.)

be, for the existence of an ultimate in history would seem to constitute foreclosure upon the future, dogmatic restraint upon the present, and indifference to the instructive heritage of the past. I have no expectation of eradicating any absurdity which is intrinsic to the Christian faith. I do expect to show, however, how it comes about that Christians and non-Christians alike impute to Christianity absurdities which are not really there, and how these absurdities may evaporate and give way to solidly redemptive meaning when the question of Christian understanding is rigorously set within the logic of history.

CHAPTER 1

REASON IN NATURE AND HISTORY

To see a thing we must adjust our visual apparatus in a certain way. If the adjustment is inadequate the thing is seen indistinctly or not at all. Take a garden seen through a window. . . . To see the garden and to see the windowpane are two incompatible operations which exclude one another because they require different adjustments.

ORTEGA Y GASSET, *The Dehumanization of Art*, Doubleday Anchor Books, 1956, pp. 9, 10.

It is doubtful whether the modes of being (being as nature, being as history) represent 'species' in the 'genus' being.

MARTIN HEIDEGGER, *An Introduction to Metaphysics*, translated by Ralph Manheim, Yale University Press, 1959, p. 81.

THE context underlying the discussion of the rationality of faith has shifted radically in recent years. Traditionally, the words "reason" and "faith" have been functions of two quite distinct contexts, nature and the supernatural. If faith were regarded as the instrument for receiving supernatural truth, and reason the instrument for receiving natural truth, every effort of the reason to know the supernatural without the aid of faith could be made to seem like an act of cosmic rebellion. When men are tempted with the suggestion that they shall be "as gods, knowing," authorship of the project is usually attributed to the serpent. However, when the "first modern man," Marlowe's Dr. Faustus, heard the temptation, it was on the lips of an angel, and Faustus gladly yielded, saying, "Here, Faustus, try thy brains to gain a deity!"

The traditional Christian has generally been satisfied with the humbler role, accepting on faith and simply trusting, without requiring that he know. But something in his spirit militates against that role. No one having seen the proud eyes of the Renaissance man is satisfied to be symbolized by the beatific submissiveness of wise virgins. "Modern man" would rather support Prometheus, wresting the fires of knowledge from the gods. He will no longer be intimidated by the insinuation that his Prometheus bears the name of Cain.

The customary context for understanding the relation between reason and faith, however, has not relaxed the tension between them.[1] Therefore, one should welcome the announcement that the

[1] That is evident in Etienne Gilson's description of the five families in the medieval church, mobilized around very different understandings of the relation of faith and reason, and in H. Richard Niebuhr's extension of the very same pattern of disagreement to the contemporary scene in his analysis of the different relations between Christ and culture. The five families represent live options today and produce quite different types of Christian piety. See *Reason and Revelation in the Middle Ages*, the James W. Richard Lectures for 1937, Scribners, 1938; and *Christ and Culture*, Harper, 1953.

context underlying the discussion has changed. One ought no longer to juxtapose nature and supernature, but nature and history.[2] This new context is jointly sponsored by the human sciences and the theological sciences. The human sciences refuse to embrace the talents of man under the single rubric of nature, for man is also an historical being. The theological sciences are increasingly reluctant to embrace the exploits of God under the rubric of supernature, for where the God of the Bible acts, there is history. In history the Promethean spirit may satisfy its passions without violating the holy of holies, because history is man's proper home. Likewise, in history the spirit of religious fidelity may experience its enlightenment without negating its fundamental humanity, for history is the tabernacle of God.

The optimism in this new base of negotiation between reason and faith is shortlived, however, when one realizes that both terms continue to be used incautiously even in the new context. To the natural reason the historical reason often resembles faith more than reason. In the setting of the faith-acts of historical thought, the faith-acts of natural thought often resemble reason more than faith. When the historical reason by immersing itself in the recorded life of its country begins to foster a spirit of patriotism, the natural reason chastens it for its fideistic headiness and calls it back to the more objective canon of factuality. On the other hand, when faith is historicized, preferring kerygmatic acts and sayings to nature miracles and cosmological myths, the naturalized faith initiates proceedings designed to expose this trend as gnosticism, docetism, or other forms of treason against a durable Christian substance. In other words, the contradictions between faith and reason are persisting even after the notable shift away from the context of nature and supernature to the context of nature and history.

[2] To stop at this juncture to say why this shift has been justifiable is unnecessary inasmuch as my whole effort is to show precisely that. For a detailed historical discussion of how the shift came about, see Friedrich Gogarten, *Demythologizing and History*, Scribners, 1955.

I. TWO STRUCTURES OF REALITY

Nature and history are structures in reality so fundamentally different that it ought to be said they have nothing in common. They are incommensurable. Conflict between them is impossible. Therefore, mediation between them is not only inachievable but superfluous. Yet, this difference, when unheeded, can become the source of the most painful fissures, chasms which exist not side by side benignly but through the middle of one's active life.

The consequence in the life of Christianity of heedlessness toward the cleavage between nature and history is most pathetic. One of the more conspicuous among them is the constant tension between the claims of reason and the claims of faith. What if there were a reason appropriate to nature and a reason appropriate to history, a faith appropriate to nature and a faith appropriate to history? And what if history were a context as different from nature as one space of a chessboard is different from another? What, then, if a believer were asked about the rationality of his faith? He could answer by simultaneously invoking history's faith and nature's reason. In that case, he would be answering with Tertullian and Kierkegaard, "What has reason to do with faith! I believe what is absurd." He would be justified, considering the connotation of his terms. The Athens of nature has nothing to do with the Jerusalem of history. But what if one were to answer the same question by simultaneously invoking history's faith and history's reason? That is, what if one were to seek his standards of validity (reason) in the same medium in which he finds his meaning as a man (faith), in history alone? In that case he could no longer support the purported fideism of Tertullian and Kierkegaard, for reason and faith do not fight in the context of history as they do when one term takes its stance in nature and the other in history. Confessions of faith tend to sound absurd when transferred from the structure of history, where they originate, to the structure of nature, where they are alien. Left in history, however, while they may not achieve complete rational transparency, the likelihood of their being absurd is totally eliminated.

In the sixteenth century, André Vesalius, a Belgian physiologist working in Italy, published a book *On the Structure of the Human Body.* There he reported that after minute inspection of the body of a man he found no trace of a missing rib. Why is it, then, that from the simplest believing Christian to the most sophisticated Christian scholar the story of creation in the Book of Genesis nonetheless remains intact? Because the phenomenon which Vesalius isolated has no bearing upon the claim that God created woman. When Vesalius cut cadavers he was dealing with nature. When the Jahwist wrote Genesis 2 he was dealing with history. These two structures of reality do not fight, because they have nothing in common. For the same reason, when the life-sciences announce they are a short step from "creating" life, they do not stagger the religious faith in God as "creator." If that event ever occurs, scientist and theologian should be able to welcome it without collision. The scientist may say, "Man can now create life," and the theologian may say, "God creates life." The two sentences can stand side by side without contradiction. The word "create" in the theologian's sentence does not point to the same structure of reality as the word "create" in the scientist's sentence. The scientist points to nature, the theologian to history, and these two structures have nothing in common.

Patience is easily strained by this apparently brittle and inflexible juxtaposition of nature and history. A much more precise definition of the terms is needed. When John Dewey defined the word "nature,"[3] he said of it, "Few terms used in philosophy have a wider or looser use, or involve greater ambiguity." If Dewey had been referring to popular understandings of the word, one could easily appreciate his sense of ambiguity. One speaks alike of the "nature" of God and the "nature" of the solar system, the "nature" of personality and the birdviewer's "nature." In philosophically controlled speech, however, the connotation of the word "nature" has enjoyed remarkable continuity. In terms of how nature is known (that is, in epistemological terms) Immanuel Kant called it "the world of possible experience." He meant that nature is what

[3] *Baldwin Dictionary of Philosophy and Psychology*, 1939.

is objectively perceivable, where science therefore can work. For, as Karl Jaspers is fond of saying in the Kantian lineage, "Science cannot proceed in the absence of an object." In terms of what nature is in its being (that is, in ontological terms) it refers to the rational structure of reality. As such the term embraces not only the realm of things, called "objective qualities as independent realities of the external world." It also embraces the realm which metaphysicians probe, the realm of essences, called "the permanent constitution of things." Isaac Newton's question, "How does light behave?", is different from Aristotle's question, "What is light?", but the difference is not great. One question is experimental and the other ontological, but both point to the natural structure of reality, insofar as neither originates in the question, "What is man?"

Nature, then, can be said to be the *structure of reality exterior to and silent about man.* That definition integrates the two elemental characteristics of nature, applicable alike to the brute things of the physical world and to the socalled things-in-themselves of the metaphysical world. The first is that nature is the realm in which "man has no special place of privilege" (Paul Ricoeur) because the question of the meaning of human life is not raised. Life with nature is thus a life of *self*-forgetfulness, a life which, like some abstract art, deliberately eliminates all human elements. The second characteristic of nature places the responsibility for this structure of reality upon man himself, for nature is an attribute of man's approach to reality. Nature is the human distance from the world resulting from man's measuring it (Martin Heidegger). Nature is therefore the structure of a reality which man cannot enter into personally because he has already held it off at an impersonal distance. Distributed in space (Schiller and Schelling), classifiable from the outside (R. G. Collingwood), therefore over against us, we can only enter into the reality of nature theoretically, without any consciousness of ourselves.

Some historians are willing to accept the structure of nature as descriptive of the structure of history as well. When they do, they are engaging in history as though it were nature. The Germans call that *Historie*. However, to engage in history as history is to expose the reality for which the word *Geschichte* is reserved. In refusing to honor this distinction, historians contribute not only to methodological confusion but to one of the fundamental elements in the crisis of our culture, which is the habit of considering reality in abstraction from its meaning for man.

History is the structure of reality interior to and vocal about man. Like nature, it is a realm where objects exist as products of organized subjects. Unlike nature, it is a realm where everything has meaning for man and exists in virtue of its meaning for man. Indeed, history by definition is the existence which alone can have meaning for man. Compare then the geometrical lines of abstract art in its effort to create a world without man to the writhing bodies of Michelangelo and even the contorted lines of Baroque art, emerging at a time when the self-consciousness of man begins to shape a dominantly human world. There the distance between reality and man is in the process of being eliminated through man's sensitive probing for a life of meaning. There abstract spaces give way to concrete times—not the time chronometers measure, which is the time of spaces, as on calendar and watch, but the time of lived reality, a time not measurable because one cannot stand outside it without destroying it. Nature, like mathematics, lends itself to systematization; history, like art, resists it.

Contemporary thinkers who are familiar with this distinction between nature and history are generally ready to accept it, although not radically. However, the distinction remains a mere aesthetic tool without significantly altering one's discernment unless it is radically applied. To apply the distinction radically means to understand that nature and history are immiscible structures. One cannot enjoy both simultaneously. Nor can one move from one to the other smoothly, without a leap. Nature and history are not dimensions which, though methodologically separate, nevertheless interpenetrate. They are poles apart in man and tend to rend his life interiorly. They are theaters of action which intersect the life of man, yet which man can attend only one at a time.

The distinction between nature and history is based on the discovery that the structure which appears when the human consciousness separates itself from things is a different structure of reality from that which appears when the consciousness joins itself to things, seeing itself in relation to them and asking the question of fundamental meaning. The separation was made in its cleanest form by Descartes in the seventeenth century when he described the *cogito* (the thinking self) in distinction from the *res extensa* (things extended in space). That distinction simply articulated what working scientists had already discovered as the ingredient basic to their laboratory methods. Science can only proceed with its method of bringing reality to appearance when it eliminates a certain kind of intrusive subjectivity and allows the uncompromised object to appear. Descartes' *Discourse on Method* may in that sense be called the first "critique of the natural reason."

At the same time, Descartes' analysis inspired the advent of the historical consciousness. By stressing the importance of isolating the object, he intensified public awareness of the subject. Not that he himself esteemed that awareness. In fact, he held history in contempt as the sphere in which imagination was king. Thanks to Descartes' analysis, however, at least two among his contemporaries seized upon the subjective pole of the subject-object dichotomy to develop a "critique of the historical reason." I refer to Pierre Bayle in France and Giambattista Vico in Italy. In his *Historical and Critical Dictionary* Bayle showed how the subjective conditions which Descartes held away from the objective in order to let nature appear were the very conditions which made for another structure of reality, called history. Some years later in his *New Science* Vico deepened this critique by showing how meditation upon history and its subjective, human character could reveal a kind of truth not available through the geometrical, objectivistic metaphysics of the Cartesian project.[4]

[4] These backgrounds are presented in a very complete way in two important works: Hans-Georg Gadamer, *Wahrheit und Methode*, Grundzüge einer philosophischen Hermeneutik, Tübingen, 1960, especially pp. 1-38 on "The

In opposing history to nature in this way one obviously does not mean by nature what romanticists and God-intoxicated writers meant. They identified nature with creation. Thus they regarded God as an historian who writes his will in the language of nature as readily as he does in the language of history. The prophetic tradition of the Old Testament is a shock to that trend, for in the prophetic point of view "the divine will has created no symbol of itself in nature" (Ernst Cassirer). Nevertheless, reality as the language of God, if that language involves the meaning of man, would not be reality as nature but as history, even if it pertained to such otherwise unmistakably "natural" phenomena as mountains and seas, deserts and gardens. One ought not say as Socrates did (*Phaedrus* 230 C) that "landscapes and trees teach us nothing," but only that if and when they do inform us about the fundamental meaning of human existence, they are not in those moments classifiable as nature but as history.

One of my most sympathetic antagonists, Professor Langdon Gilkey, once suggestively criticized this distinction between nature and history by insisting that on board ship he has often found more meaning on deck alone with the sea and the stars than in the public lounge engaged by people. He meant to show that nature, too—the stars and the sea—is a structure of reality in which meaning can be experienced, whereas in history—peopled places—one can experience complete dearth of meaning. The illustration is helpful in demonstrating what a specialized connotation I intend for "nature" and "history." Nature is the structure of reality in which the question of meaning is not raised. Therefore, peopled places *can* be nature. History is the structure of reality where the question of meaning is raised. Therefore, being in the presence of stars and the sea *can* be history. When this is understood, it can

Meaning of the Humanistic Tradition for the Human Sciences" (die Geisteswissenschaften); and Georges Gusdorf, *Introduction aux Sciences Humaines*, Essai critique sur leurs origines et leur développement, Paris, 1960, especially Part II, Chapter III, "The Appearance of the Idea of Nature," and Part III, Chapter V, "The Awakening of the Historical Sense."

be seen that nature in its popular, nature-lore, Psalmnody definition—as birds, bees, skies and seas—cannot be simply an "arena" which God has created within which man works out his historical destiny. That would truly be the impoverishment of nature, reducing it to a subhuman tool for human and divine enterprises. The things around us, ordinarily called nature, have their own historical significance. They are dehistoricized only when meaningful communion with them is interrupted by making them objects of detached investigation—as men must if they are to subdue the earth.

Therefore, to define nature as a dehistoricized structure of reality is not a device for shrinking nature to nothing and letting history alone prevail. That trend also was apparent in Romanticism. Revolt against the mathematical world of the emerging modern science prevented the romanticist from appreciating nature as a structure of reality legitimately independent from historical reality. A comparable blindness to nature as objective methods of research define it is evident today in the thought of some existentialists, and for the same reason. They wrongly deny man the right to approach reality without raising the question about its meaning for man, which is the question in which the historical structure originates. Therefore "nature" for them tends to take on the pejorative characteristics once attributed to the material world by gnostics and manichaeans.

The major force of the distinction, then, is neither to redeem nature through history, nor to condemn nature for being a-historical. The distinction bears primarily upon the meaning of rationality. Awareness of the distinction has the merit of advising, indeed of warning that investigations which began with the structure of nature will never arrive at realities which reside in the structure of history. There can be no smooth continuity between nature and history because such continuity would itself require the mediation of man. Yet, depending upon his method of mediation, man is always participating either in nature or in history and not in both at the same time. Such a demand, then, would not be a demand for continuity between two different kinds of objects in space and time, natural objects and historical objects, although that is how common sense visualizes the problem, to the great jeopardy of precise understanding. The demand would rather call for continuity between two different kinds of human relation to reality. To call for continuity under those conditions is asking for the impossible. History vainly feeds on nature as a character in an Ionesco play vainly devours crusts of bread to fill the gaps in his memory.

The distinction between nature and history is not a distinction between two different kinds of reality but between two different structures of reality, two different orders of constructs. The judgment about the dichotomy of nature and history, therefore, while it may have metaphysical and ontological implications, is a methodological judgment. The dichotomy, therefore, is methodological. That fact ought not detract from the serious consequences attendant upon making the dichotomy unwittingly. The easy assumption that reality remains one and the same irrespective of the modes of our relationship is ruinous both to rational clarity and to personal authenticity. One cannot assume that reality is "out there" in such a way that, notwithstanding the different approaches called "nature" and "history," reality is nonetheless undivided and continuous.

In the mountains, for instance, there are two different sorts of recreational operations. One is to walk the paths, the other is to climb the peaks. Walking and climbing both involve the use of the legs. Anyone who has experienced both modes of ambulation would regard it as a dangerous banality, however, to assume that "legs" remain the same reality in the transition from walking to climbing. A mountain climber, like a tightrope walker, is in a sickening struggle face to face with death. That posture radically alters the structure of reality as it may otherwise be experienced in more pedestrian moments. In the same sense, nature and history are not species of some common reality underlying them as a genus under which they are subsumed. Nature and history are immiscible structures of reality. Why, then, should it be supposed that theological quests begun in objective detachment should be dealing with the same reality upon which one focuses who initiates his quest in the passion of personal concern?

Likewise, and even more significantly, the assumption that the self remains one and the same, notwithstanding the modes of its relation to reality, goes unchallenged at the jeopardy of personal integrity. Nature is a structure characterized by I-it relations. History is a structure characterized by I-thou relations. From Martin Buber's famous analysis it is fairly obvious that "I-it" and "I-thou" are quite different structures of reality, even when the apparent object of the relation of both egos bears the same name in both relations. The mountain peak called "Matterhorn" may be "it" or "thou," depending on one's mode of relation to it. The fact that it is always "there," in the same place, subject to the same exterior tests and measures, does not guarantee that it is the same kind of reality when measured as it is when mounted. That much has always been patent in Martin Buber's dichotomy.

What is not so obvious to the casual devotee of the Buber thesis is that not only the object changes in the movement from one structure to the other, but the subject changes as well. The I in the I-it relation is not the same I as the I in the I-thou relation. The subject is not self-evidently continuous through all its states. The possibility for continuity in selves is an historical possibility and not a physical or metaphysical possibility. The dichotomy between nature and history is as devastating to the quality of selves as it is to the quality of external realities. That is why the oscillation between methods of nature and methods of history has a crucial bearing upon the very reality of personal existence. Why then should it be supposed that theological quests begun in objective detachment leave the questing person in no different position of selfhood than those which originate in the passion of personal concern? As Kierkegaard has said, one notices when he has lost a job, or an arm, or a wife, but the loss of one's self generally goes undetected. Consider the poem of Kenneth Rexroth. A fashion model has so exteriorized herself into the clothes in which she poses, that when she undresses at night the self which she assumed was always there beneath her clothes is gone and she is forced to wear her clothes to bed in order to keep intact whatever self remains. On May 3, 1913, Franz Kafka expressed this very possibility in one phrase in his diary: "The terrible uncertainty of my inner existence."

Because the structures of nature and history are constituted in two quite different types of human relation, it is a sophism to assert that while nature is not the sufficient cause of history it is the necessary cause. Are canvas and oils the necessary though not sufficient cause of a work of art? To say "cause" is to say "constant antecedent." Are canvas and oil the constant antecedent of a work of art, and nature the constant antecedent of history? Indeed, rather, canvas and oil molded plastically into a symbolic form *are* the work of art. They are no longer canvas and oil.

A distress signal flashed from a mountain is decoded as a message about some human emergency. The light is obviously not the sufficient cause of the message but is it not the necessary cause? Indeed, rather, the message is both the sufficient and the necessary cause of the light, or—better said—the message and the light are indistinguishably fused by the person communicating the message.[5] In the same way, the constant antecedent of historical realities must be sought in history, not in nature.

A constant antecedent of history which is itself properly historical is more apt to be called a motive than a cause. History is a reality which always embraces states of consciousness. Causes, which may produce states of consciousness, do not persist in the states they produce, hence do not adequately account for history. Motives do, however. Motives are unquestionably historical in

[5] Cf. Kenneth Mark Colby, "Research in Psychoanalytic Information Theory," in *American Scientist*, Vol. 49, No. 3, Sept. 1961, pp. 366, 367. The illustration is used in clarification of the following position: "As a clinical and experimental psychoanalyst, as a practical man, I am an unashamed dualist. . . . I consider mind and brain to involve two quite different orders of constructs, two different kinds of observations and two different sorts of operations on phenomena." I am indebted to Professor John Ollom, Drew University department of physics, for calling my attention to this article.

structure as causes are not, allowing history to be explained by history rather than by nature.[6] To distinguish between nature and history in this radical way is not meant to deny the influence of the structure of nature upon the structure of history. It is only to insist that the structures are so distinct that statements about nature are never to be confused with statements about history, whatever their relation to each other may be. When a congressman, slated to give an important address, calls the speaker of the House to announce, "I have the grippe," and the speaker replies, "Take an aspirin and go to bed," the congressman can feel insulted. What seemed to him an historically significant disease has been treated as a matter of nature. If he calls his doctor to make the same announcement and the doctor says, "Too bad! You'll miss your address!" he may at first feel flattered, but after a moment's reflection he will recall the doctor to his clinical duty. Even if the doctor proceeds on the theory that the disease has been brought on by anxiety over the address, thus suggesting that not all of nature is easily walled off from all of history, he may be treating the congressman in no less natural terms. That is, the use of historical understanding in the therapy of diseases may not be an historical operation. More certainly, statements about nature, while they may under certain circumstances settle historical questions, are not themselves historical statements.[7]

In the Christian faith, the constant antecedent of the cross is not a geological formation called Golgotha but Jesus' obedience to the word of God. The antecedent of the resurrection is not the empty tomb but Jesus' obedience, victorious over the powers of

[6] Cf. Ortega y Gasset, *The Dehumanization of Art*, Anchor Book, 1956, pp. 25 and 26, note 6.

[7] Cf. Erwin Panofsky, *Meaning in the Visual Arts*, Anchor Book, 1955, p. 15: "A statement to the effect that the pigments used in an allegedly mediaeval miniature were not invented before the nineteenth century may settle an art-historical question, but it is not an art-historical statement. Based as it is on chemical analysis plus the history of chemistry, it refers to the miniature not *qua* work of art but *qua* physical object, and may just as well refer to a forged will."

the world. The antecedent of the divine sonship of Jesus of Nazareth was not some genetic irregularity but God's word to his people fulfilled in the ear of Mary. In the same way one can say that the necessary cause of the apostolic faith is the historical Jesus, if by historical Jesus is meant the event of Jesus of Nazareth interpreting his acts through his words and not the raw factuality of this man as an object in space and time. Why are the antecedents of explosions different from the antecedents of wars? One who knows that will know why nature cannot be the antecedent of history. Why is the action of a car skidding into a tree quite different structurally from the action of a car stopping for a pedestrian? One who knows that will know why the structure of nature is immiscible with the structure of history.[8] But is not the River Nile a necessary cause of the history of Egypt and the insularity of Great Britain a necessary cause of her imperial achievements? Insofar as that is true, rivers and islands are not natural but historical realities, as Jesus' birth in Bethlehem is an historical and not a gynecological reality and as Jesus' arrest in the garden of Gethsemane is an historical and not a horticultural reality. The lightning which drove Martin Luther into a monastery was simply not the same kind of reality which led Benjamin Franklin to the discovery of electricity.

Evidence is mounting today that scientists and philosophers are not content with so sharp a bifurcation between history and nature. Yet their efforts to penetrate this structural barrier seem unconvincing. Attention is called to how no science can proceed without a history of science, just as no doctor can make a diagnosis without a case history. However, the history referred to in that instance is a history not of a fundamentally human reality but of a fundamentally non-human reality, a history of man as object, therefore not a history at all in an eminently historical sense. Attention is also drawn to how all the instruments used by a scientist in his

[8] I have drawn these two illustrations from Raymond Aron, *Introduction to the Philosophy of History,* translated from the French of 1938 by George C. Irwin, Beacon Press, 1961, p. 185, and *Dimensions de la conscience historique,* Paris, 1961, p. 65, respectively.

laboratory for probing the reality of nature are instruments made by men, so that the approach to science is from the start humanly conditioned. Yet, these instruments designed by men are designed with the specific intention of eliminating as completely as possible the characteristic human passions from the moment of natural discovery.

The most sustained and seductive attack upon the partition between nature and history is made by the British scientist and philosopher, Michael Polanyi. His work entitled *Personal Knowledge* concerns the scientist's approach to nature and contends that the approach is inextricably personal. Natural knowledge is said to be historical because it embraces the human structure. "The I-It situation has been gradually transformed into an I-Thou relation."[9] Case after case from the history of science is paraded as evidence that the crucial moment on the way to an inductive result has either waited upon the discovery of a "subjective," "personal" factor in the total fact or has been initiated in some subjective construct.

According to Polanyi, there is some personal knowledge in every act by which science structures "nature." Personal knowledge by employing subjective passions has a logic of its own which is indispensable to science. For instance, personal guesses, which are less than knowledge because they are objectively unverified, are also more than knowledge because they are the very means by which new discoveries are made. A science which honors this personal dimension is called by Polanyi a "fiduciary science." Even in science one strives for knowledge under the guidance of "antecedent belief." Objectivism falsifies one's concept of truth by exalting what can be proved at the expense of what cannot be proved. For science, therefore, objective detachment is a myth.

Often what Polanyi calls a personal factor is some lag or some distortion in the perceptual responses of the experimenter. When these responses are included in the data of observations, they turn

[9] *Op. cit.*, p. 346, Chicago, 1958. Cf. John Herman Randall, Jr., *Nature and Historical Experience*, New York, 1958, p. 61: "Objectivity means always being objective for something."

out to be no more human or personal than the variation of the temperature within the laboratory or the change of air pressure in a tube. Polanyi's personal knowledge is not history but the observation of nature in its separation from history, even though that observation includes man as active, imaginative, courageous observer. That is, personal knowledge which begins in subjective passions or private standpoints is not personal knowledge in the sense in which historical knowledge is personal. It is disqualified not simply because it ends, as Polanyi knows, in objective validation. It is disqualified because it does not begin in the properly personal question, the question about the fundamental meaning of life. Therefore, while Polanyi's work may be an excellent antidote to the myth of positivism in natural science it is not a possibility for bridging the methodological chasm between nature and history.

The work of Ernst Cassirer had already developed the convictions Polanyi expresses, and with greater philosophical awareness. Science, according to Cassirer, deals not with material objects themselves but with perceptions. Unlike things, perceptions belong to persons. The creative action of the mind in bringing the material world into expression places before the scientist not a world of objects but a human world, a world of "meaning." Scientific knowledge is symbolic knowledge and involves forms of the human understanding. Immanuel Kant long ago discerned this from the way Newton worked. Every startling observation of natural processes has begun in an artful intellectual model. The planet Neptune, for example, was anticipated in theory long before it was observed in fact. Scientists do not wait passively for objects to impress themselves. Symbols created by their active intellect initiate the exposure of nature. The way things are related to each other is not the same as the way things are related to a man. For a man intuits not simply by the senses but also by the use of categories of understanding in his intelligence.[10]

[10] In America, Professor Harold K. Schilling is developing the same essential understanding of scientific knowledge and demonstrating its similarity to methods of religious understanding. His position has the virtues and the limitations of Cassirer's. See Ernst Cassirer, *The Philosophy of Symbolic*

However, the self-knowledge which Cassirer and Kant found implicit in every scientific cognition does not at all resemble the self-knowledge extolled by Socrates' oracle. The self which participates in structuring the world of nature is not the same self which demands that life be significant. Symbolic forms to be historically significant and thus to clarify the faith and understanding of historical religions must originate in the question of the meaning of man and not simply in general forms of human appreciation. Cassirer has acknowledged this quite explicitly in his *Essay on Man* where he says, "We must forget man in order to study nature. . . . In the development of scientific thought the anthropomorphic element is progressively forced into the background until it entirely disappears in the ideal structure of physics. History proceeds in a quite different way. It can live and breathe only in the human world."[11]

Many do not see how the human subject can in any way be eliminated from scientific investigation because they do not see that there are two subjects, the subject which constitutes objects by its mental constructs, such as by laws of nature, and the subject which participates in objects according to their human meaning. Natural scientists know the importance of this distinction between subjectivities when they refuse to describe a color by such a humanly relative title as "red." Blind and color-blind men do not see "red." That need not affect the universality and objectivity of the color. The physical language for that reality is the wave length of the radiation reflected from the surface of the colored object. In nature, all men, despite their relative, subjective, sensory contact with the object, may have an identical appreciation of it. That is the deliberate aim of scientists in working with the structure of nature. "They aim at abstracting from the whole world of

---

Forms, Yale University Press, Vol. I, 1953 (translated from the German of 1923 by Ralph Manheim), pp. 73-114; Vol. III, 1957 (from the German of 1929), pp. 45-57. Cf. Schilling's *Science and Religion:* An Interpretation of Two Communities, Scribners, 1962.

[11] Yale University Press, New Haven, 1944, p. 191.

reality that part which is truly objective in the sense that it is independent of any particular observance." That is why it can still be said, despite Polanyi, Cassirer, and others, that the "conceptual distinction between objective and subjective reality is one of the greatest achievements of our western civilization."[12]

II. THE TRANSITION FROM NATURE TO HISTORY

The form of rationality known today as historical understanding is born in the transition from the structure of nature to the structure of history. It is important to say "in the transition" because historical understanding is in jeopardy when it loses the consciousness that it might again become natural understanding. Nature is not a solid reality which is there prior to and foundational to history, to which history need constantly return. Nature is there rather as a warning as to how tempting it is for man to think on one plane only. Nor are nature and history simply two ways of experiencing some third reality lurking in the background. Count von Yorck and Wilhelm Windelband, two pioneers in the nuancing of the nature-history relation, conceded that nature and history were "moments of one experience despite their disparateness."[13] In this they yielded to the drive toward monism which dominated Hegel as it has most of the history of philosophy. For Hegel the duality of nature and history was sufficiently dichotomous to be referred to as the "unhappy consciousness." Contradiction was of its essence. Yet he resolved the dichotomy. "The truth of this process," he said, "is precisely that this doubled consciousness is one."[14]

Wilhelm Dilthey, however, has been the chief methodologist

[12] Reginald O. Kapp, *Towards a Unified Cosmology*, London, 1960, p. 178. William Temple had referred to the same distinction as "the most disastrous moment in the history of Europe."

[13] Fritz Kaufmann, "Die Philosophie des Grafen Paul Yorck von Wartenburg," *Jahrbuch für Philosophie und phänomenologische Forschung*, 1928, Volume IX, p. 44; and Bernard Erling, *Nature and History*, A Study in Theological Methodology with Special Attention to the Method of Motif Research, Lund, 1960, pp. 41 and 240 on Windelband.

[14] *Phänomenologie des Geistes*, Hoffmeister edition, p. 160.

in the backgrounds of the contemporary "critique of the historical reason." He is distinguished for his refusal of the compromise with traditional philosophy. Contemporary phenomenologists and existentialists follow him in this. Their joint importance for the question of rationality is that they see nature and history not as two moments of one experience, or two slants on what is fundamentally the same event, but as two structural moments of reality itself. Historical understanding is born when one becomes aware of history as the sole structure in which man lives with meaning.

The importance of the distinction between nature and history is its clarification of what is meant by rationality. One of the most provocative statements in contemporary thought sharpens the distinction instructively. Martin Heidegger has said in his book, *Was heisst Denken?*, "Science doesn't think." He might have said, "The *scientist* doesn't think," by which, of course, he would have meant, "The scientist *as* scientist." "Think" is a function word, and Heidegger seems intent on denying the word to the structure of nature. Aristotle hinted at the same claim when he said, "If there are any entities or substances such as the dialecticians say the ideas are, there must be something much more scientific than science itself" (*Metaphysics* 1050b, 35-37). Pascal directed a similar statement against Descartes in saying, "The science of things exterior will not console me for my ignorance of morality in time of affliction." Kant's movement from the pure reason to the practical reason was dictated by the same sense of the ultimate futility of a "scientific" approach to life. "Natural experience tells us what exists," he said, "but it does not tell us that what exists ought to exist precisely as it does exist and not differently; that is why natural experience does not give the universal truth, and that is why the reason which aspires avidly to this kind of knowledge is more irritated than satisfied by experience."[15] Husserl's thinking is most immediately in the backgrounds of Heidegger's understanding: "Daily practical living is naïve. . . . Nor is it otherwise in the

[15] Cited from *The Critique of Pure Reason* by Enrico Castelli, *Les Présupposés d'une Théologie de l'Historie, Paris,* 1954, p. 78.

positive sciences. They are naïvetés of a higher level. They are the products of an ingenious theoretical technique; but the intentional performances from which everything ultimately originates remain unexplicated."[16]

Heidegger unveiled the mystery of his curious statement when he asked the German physicist, C. F. von Weizsäcker, if *he* believed that science thinks. Von Weizsäcker's reply was almost equally as diverting as the question. "No, science does not think," he said, "it knows." However, he went on to say, "Science also believes. . . . It believes in the regularity of nature and it is rooted in this belief as firmly as a religious belief is rooted in a system of religion." Heidegger seemed pleased with the response, for it gave him the occasion to reveal what he himself had all along meant. Science does not think, he said, because by its methods science cannot say what it *means* by "laws of nature" and other such articles of faith informing its methods. Merleau-Ponty seemed to have the same limit of science in mind when he said, "A science without philosophy literally would not know what it is talking about," or Raymond Aron when he said of syphilis, according to the law of sequence "it brings on general paralysis, but we do not understand it."[17]

These judgments by philosophers directed at natural science should not be construed as depreciating the scientific enterprise. One would hope they are not even meant to encourage scientists to mix metaphysics and faith with their objective tools. Science can proceed without a metaphysics and without a faith. Nor is it the work of a science to know what is *meant* by laws of nature so long as laws of nature work for the sciences. It is enough that a science "knows" what it is talking about as a science without asking it to "know what it is talking about" as a philosophy. In the context of Heidegger's connotation of "think" Ernest Hemingway was

[16] *Cartesian Meditations,* An Introduction to Phenomenology, trans. by Dorion Cairns, The Hague, 1960, pp. 152, 153.

[17] Merleau-Ponty, *Sens et Non-Sens,* Paris, 1948, p. 171; Aron, *Introduction to the Philosophy of History,* p. 46.

right to have his doctor, Rinaldi, say in *Farewell to Arms,* "I don't think, I operate." Camus was right to have his doctor, Rieux, say in *The Plague,* "A man can't cure and *know* at the same time."

An adequate comprehension of rationality demands that its claims be limited to its craft and that some single function-word like "think" not to be asked to serve alike in all contexts of reality. Reason and rationality are functions of contexts and their meanings shift when the contexts shift. If there are two structures of reality and not just one, then the question of rationality which depends upon structures will always be equivocally answered unless the context of its claims is announced. Hegel was as provocative as Heidegger when he said in almost the same terms, "The I . . . does not think."[18] Nature for Hegel was the structure of reality which emerges when an I stands opposite an object in an act of theoretical contemplation. That act cannot be called thinking in the same sense as thinking which evinces an interest in the fundamental meaning of the self, as, for instance, the thinking of an historian when he immerses himself in the world with the deliberate intention of estimating its bearing upon things human.[19]

The rationality which emerges when history is allowed its distinctness from nature is of a very precise sort. When the Christian faith in particular is interpreted within the structure of history, the implications for its rationality are utterly decisive. To illustrate, I will select two areas where faithfulness to historical interpretation is most difficult to achieve yet most imperative, namely, creation and resurrection.

A. CREATION AS HISTORY ALONE

What is the precise rationality of the belief that "God created the world"?

[18] *Phenomenology of Mind,* J. B. Baillie translation, The Macmillan Co., p. 150; cf. also pp. 242, 243.

[19] The discussion between Heidegger and von Weizsäcker occurred at a meeting of Marburg University alumni in 1959.

The Christian doctrine of creation is the doctrine most likely to be expressed in the categories of nature. When that is done, it is customarily interpreted in this way:

"World": the things around us, subject to subdivision, weight, and measure; the surface on which history customarily glides; the magnitude which lends itself to inspection by technical instruments, but which can also be appreciated aesthetically without such mediation.

"God": invisible cause or source of all visible reality, omniscient, omnipotent, omnipresent, eternal. That list of attributes was taught the Christian church not by the prophets and apostles but by the philosophers of antiquity who were in the thrall alternately of materialistic and idealistic categories, both dominated by the structure of nature. Far from being historical in the sense in which the witness of the Bible is historical, they deal with the reality of God as an object, separated from man, who works upon the world with technological means, and with whom therefore meaningful relationship of the sort that characterizes man's domain is neglected.

"Creation": an act performed by God at the beginning of time, or, a beginning which is the source and explanation of all reality.

In Christianity, the meaning of creation ought to be expressed in a fundamentally different way. Western thought has accustomed the church to treating creation as a cosmological myth which explains the existence of the universe. That way of thinking has appealed to religious sentiment because it has usually been found clothed in reverently agnostic language. Yet, in that regard the Biblical faith is not different from the philosophical faith of the Rig-veda. In Christianity, however, the doctrine of creation has to do not with cosmology but with history, not with the temporal origin nor with the technical explanation of the universe but with the meaning of man's life.

One cannot deny that the Bible and the creeds of the Church make statements about the cosmos. However, these statements are almost always made in the service of history, for they intend to conserve the meaning of God's activity with man. Therefore, if analysts treat the cosmological statements of the faith cosmologically, they do these statements exegetical violence. In the work of interpretation statements must not be isolated from the structures which gave rise to them. When the Hebrew fathers and prophets say God has chosen Israel as a light to the Gentiles, the meaning of this event is expressed in the familiar story of creation. By this story one means to confess that the God who has chosen Israel is the Lord of the universe, and no mere local deity. He is the most high God, sovereign of all, and he has chosen a people through whom to mediate his relationship to the entire world. When twentieth-century Christians find in the Bible statements about creation, they must not read them in detachment from this original historical intention. The statements do not point to the structure of nature in its independence from man but to man in his responsibility to God. They are not teachings about the cosmos but a way of saying how a singular people like the Jews can be the bearer of divine grace. The historical intention in the Christian doctrine of creation is the same, namely, that man's life does not derive its meaning from the world but from its relationship to God.

In this framework of historical interpretation the statement that "God created the world" contains an entirely different kind of rationality than appears when the nature-history dichotomy is overlooked.

"God": the reality we know as sovereign of all reality through the way he has chosen to reveal himself in history, making covenants with a people and expressing himself finally in Jesus of Nazareth. As Luther made clear, the omnipotence of God is not a category of nature, for it does not mean that God can do anything. It is a category of grace, which means God's deeds are as they are interpreted through his word.[20]

[20] Cited from *The Bondage of the Will* by Friedrich Gogarten, *Die Verkündigung Jesu Christi,* Heidelberg, 1948, p. 531.

"Creation": the historical act in which God gives the world to man, an act of such essential meaningfulness that man's life is placed within a structure which makes it possible to say of him, he has a history.

"World": where man's life is organized by meaning, either the meaning of faith, which is acceptance of the world from God, or the meaning of revolt, which defines man's search for meaning by rejection of God's acts in history.

In the structure of nature, the question of creation begins with the existence of a world. This reverses the way in which the understanding of creation entered the Hebrew-Christian tradition. Biblically, the question of a world begins in the understanding of the redemptive activity of God in history, and the belief in creation is a theological exposition of that activity.

This division between nature and history with respect to creation comes within a hair's breadth of reintroducing the Marcionite heresy. Marcionism in the early church was the teaching that the God of the New Testament was not the creator of the world. An evil God, the God of the Old Testament, was responsible for making the world. The position had remarkable insight, for it showed a possible way for Christians to receive the world from God—through his love expressed in the New Testament—without accepting everything in the world as if God intended it. But Marcionism was wrong on two counts. First, Marcionism was wrong to take the Old Testament statements about creation as cosmological, as explanations of the natural world. In that mistake, Marcion had the company of most of early Christendom. Mainly, however, Marcionism was wrong to allow two bases for interpreting the universe, an evil and a good. The Biblical faith is irrevocably monotheistic, which means there can be only one source from which to receive the world, one standpoint of interpretation. In the structure of nature the universe is explained but it is not *interpreted.* Interpretation is the function of the structure of history. In history there is only one God, hence only one principle of interpretation. The

Hebrew-Christian tradition is unanimous about that. However, when the role of explanation begins to assume the burden of interpretation, or, contrariwise, when the role of interpretation begins to function as explanation, the unity implicit in the historical, monotheistic faith is jeopardized.

In the Middle Ages, Averroes' Aristotelian view of the world as eternal was a block to the forward progress of what then functioned as the Christian doctrine of creation. Thomas Aquinas circumvented that block by demonstrating the congruity between the view of an eternally created world and the doctrine of creation. "Creation," he said, does not indicate a point of beginning but a source of dependence. Hence, even if the world had always existed, it would be no less God's "creature." Today the apologetic situation is almost the reverse. The satellite, Explorer XI, has produced data which encourages the theory that the universe had a beginning—in a vast explosion occurring some billions of years ago. If it can be said that the world had a beginning in time, have we an open gambit for the doctrine of creation as the explanation of the beginning of the universe? Will we now say more confidently than in the past that it does not matter how God did it, as long as he did it? There are basically two reasons for refusing that gambit: one, the origin of the world is explicable without reference to a doctrine of creation; and two, the doctrine of creation does not address itself to the question about the origin of the world.

The question about the origin of the world is a question of "nature." Biblical faith does not affirm that God creates "nature" but that he creates "history," and that he is Lord both of "nature" and of "history." It is mysterious to me why this way of defining nature continues to seem so bizarre to some theologians. Kant long ago called "nature" the "world of possible experience," that is, the world *man* creates when he applies himself to understanding through the laws of the speculative reason. More recently Karl Barth called "nature" the "mere 'world'—*cosmos*—but never creation." Edmund Husserl "carefully distinguished" " 'Nature' included in my ownness" from "Nature, pure and simple—that is to say: from the Nature that becomes the theme of the natural scientist." Even John Wesley used the term "nature" as I am doing in this discussion when he called one "a natural man" who "is utterly ignorant of himself" (Sermon IX). Alfred North Whitehead defined "nature" as the "physical world," meaning the world which the laws of physics isolate. The British scientist, Reginald O. Kapp, therefore, can with impunity urge his fellow scientists not to use the word "creation" because it is a theological word. Theologians ought to be able to return the compliment in using the word "nature" by declining to treat it as indicating the sphere to which the word "creation" is applicable.

When a small child reverently points to the first flower of spring and exclaims, "God made that," he need not mean by "made" what cosmologists do. He may simply be receiving the world from God, not attributing artisanship to God's activity. However, he has employed the language of artisanship, which is the language of nature. Therefore, sooner or later the incautious language of his pious mood will allow the rationality of his faith to be drawn into the structure of nature where it will collide with nature's own rationality. Through this transfiguration of language he will come to forget why it was he once said, "God made that." He might rather, therefore, have learned a language less subject to erosion into nature categories. He might have learned to express his relation to the world in some such liturgical phrase as, "All things come of thee, O Lord." In that phrase, one can learn to receive the world from God, to understand its meaning in relation to the meaning God makes present to history, without being drawn into speculation about the origin of things. This point is made for theological reasons, and not in apologetic retreat from advancing science, which is continually narrowing the range of credibility in theological statements about nature. The real pathos surrounding the doctrine of creation is not how theologians have exploited the cosmological ignorance of the Christian public by their sophisticated extension of primitive Christianity's cosmological fantasies. It is that the tactic sidetracks a candid meeting with God at the level of his redemptive intention. As John Calvin very early made plain, "To say God is the creator means we receive everything from his hands."[21]

B. RESURRECTION AS HISTORY ALONE

What, then, is the rationality of the belief that "God raised Jesus from the dead"?

Like the Biblical doctrine of creation, the Christian understanding of the resurrection of Jesus had its origin in history and not in nature. Placing the resurrection in the structure of nature one emphasizes its similarity to other resurrections, making the unique Christ-event a particular instance of the general phenomenon, "resurrection." As a natural event, it would be considered something past which affects our present the way one billiard ball affects another. Doubt of such a reality would be stubbornness, considering that the event is demonstrable in such empirical evidences as wounds in hands and side. While the "experiment" is not repeatable today, the record of eyewitnesses is considered ample proof.

One can speak in this way about the resurrection and not embrace a single proposition which illuminates man's life. That emptiness is the clue to a reality primarily natural. One does not enter into it inwardly, that is, meaningfully. Such accounts, although present in the scriptures of the church, did not appear in the earliest testimony. The consciousness of Christ's resurrection was not originally articulated in psycho-physical terms. When it did come to be included in these terms, it was in reaction to doubts of the community regarding the redemptive meaning of Jesus of Nazareth. The process of verifying historical meaning is always a process of naturalizing, and its intention is generally apologetic. What is frequently overlooked in the reading of the scriptures, however, is the way in which the scriptures conserve the resistance of the church itself to this process of naturalizing. The classic instance

[21] *Institutes*, 1536, *Opera Selecta*, Vol. I, edited by Peter Barth, Munich, 1926, p. 56.

of apologetic is the account of Jesus' showing his wounds to Thomas. The doubts of Thomas were mainly oriented to the structure of nature. The Gospel of John, chief New Testament critic of naturalizing tendencies in the early faith, opposes to this story the story of Mary in the garden. Jesus warns her, "Touch me not!" With the same motive, the Thomas story is countered by the injunction, "It is better to believe not having seen." The Gospel of Peter, which describes Christ's resurrection as a natural process, was kept out of the canonical scriptures by the early fathers. The Epistle to the Hebrews, on the other hand, shows concern to keep the faith historically oriented. The object of the faith, it reports, does involve tangible magnitudes, like Mount Sinai or the hilled city of Jerusalem. Nevertheless, it is not something that "may be touched." In the faith, Jerusalem like Mount Sinai is in no sense a geographical or geological phenomenon. It is "a voice," "a message" (Hebrews 12:18, 19). The German philosopher, Hamann, understood that distinction when he said that nature opens our eyes, but history opens our ears.

One is accustomed to saying of the creation of the world that there is no evidence for it because no one was there, not even Adam. The event was too original to be witnessed. The witness can only presuppose the event. That understanding of one's relation to creation is also true of one's relation to the resurrection of Jesus, in the sense that in the resurrection Jesus is not the object of man's faith but the source. However, if one means that the events of resurrection and creation must be exempted from the canons of understanding which are customary to history, he runs the risk of supernaturalizing them and thus of reverting to the framework in which the Christian faith is no longer historical.

Inseparable from the tendency to supernaturalize is the tendency to naturalize. In the case of belief in creation, naturalizing means to regard "creation" as an originally cosmological act, whereas it is rather postulated by faith as the presupposition of God's redemptive activity in history. The naturalizing tendency is even more seductive in respect of the resurrection, due to the significantly different structure in the testimony to the resurrection. "Resurrection" is not a simple postulate required by faith in God's redemptive activity in Jesus of Nazareth, as "creation" was a postulate of God's redemptive activity in Israel. For while the meaning of "creation" arises out of the faith of Israel, the faith of the church arises out of the meaning of "resurrection." That is to say, "resurrection" enjoys an historical priority which does not obtain for "creation." Hence one is driven to express this priority of the resurrection. What could be more suitable than some cosmological phenomenon to account for the ensuing historical faith? In such terms the resurrection becomes an act of *Deus ex machina.* One might express it this way: "The cause of Christ, which, by its failure on the cross, has left his followers in disillusionment, suddenly emerges as valid because God has certified it through the miraculous delivery of Jesus from the grave."

I am fully aware of the popular appeal in this line of reasoning and of the sophisticated support it receives within the church today. One of England's outstanding preachers stated the case for the resurrection in *The London Sunday Times* Magazine Section on Easter Sunday of 1961, under the title, "The Incredible Certainty."

> One of the fundamentals of the Christian faith (he said) is, to the modern, one of its greatest difficulties. The fundamental is that Jesus Christ survived death and proved his survival to His followers, changing them overnight from fugitive cowards to missionary martyrs. . . . For myself I am convinced that future discoveries in the field of psychic research, which man will make when he examines that field with all the scientific disciplines now used in say, physics, will illumine for us the manner of the Resurrection. Probably before Christ died, He who revealed such amazing power over other men's bodies set in motion energies in regard to His own which culminated in His finishing finally with matter as we know it and emerging from the tomb in a 'body' of a different vibration altogether.

The inadequacy of this statement manifests itself in the sensation one has while reading it that, in so appealing to the credibility of a resurrection, one's living faith in the Holy Spirit is being slowly evaporated and one is finally to be left confronting a credible ghost.

To put it blandly, the mistake in this account is to attempt to explain the resurrection in a medium in which it does not occur. Resurrection is an historical reality, and as there is no way from nature to history, naturalistic accounts do not inspire historical meaning. Apostolic testimony to the resurrection avoids the reduction of the historical faith to categories of nature, as I have indicated. It does so, however, not because it fears that the faith is incredible, and not because it lacks the scientific sophistication to make it credible, but because the credibility of the resurrection faith is of an historical order and not of a natural order. The illumination of the resurrection faith must be found in history if it is to give rise to the meanings which are history. The story of the Emmaus Road experience where the resurrected Lord appears to two travellers is placed in the Gospel account not as one more evidence of a post-resurrection fact but as testimony that one will not understand the event of the resurrection in isolation from the pre-history of which it is a part, even as Jesus taught them, "beginning with Moses and all the prophets" (Luke 24:27). The post-easter faith does not rest upon a nature miracle, because its very possibility is dependent upon a proper understanding of the pre-easter faith.[22]

[22] I have adapted Gerhard Ebeling's formulation, "The post-easter faith is known as nothing but the proper understanding of the pre-easter Jesus." (*Wort und Glaube*, Tübingen, 1960, p. 315.) Ernst Fuchs succinctly expresses the exegetical revolution inherent in that formulation when he says in the foreword of his *Zur Frage nach dem historischen Jesus*, "If formerly we interpreted the historical Jesus with the aid of the primitive Christian *kerygma*, today we interpret this *kerygma* with the aid of the historical Jesus—the two directions of the interpretation supplement each other." (Tübingen, 1960.) Probably the strongest single influence upon the current popular continental emphasis on the place of the pre-easter Jesus has been

What, then, is the resurrection in historical terms? The resurrection is the event in which it is revealed through Jesus of Nazareth who God really is and in which that revelation brings to life the new people of God, the church. In Jesus, God has given the world a future. The future is not empty, nor is it to be filled with human aspirations which are subject to the querulous scepticism of their innovators. In the resurrection Jesus ascends to his Father. The Father of Jesus is God. Henceforth, his father will be our father. That is the meaning of the resurrection which Jesus communicates to Mary in the garden. It is the meaning he instructs her to communicate to the disciples, and the message the disciples are commissioned to carry to the world. "I am ascending to my Father. Through me he is your Father" (John 20:17). Thus the promise of Jesus to his disciples in his farewell address is fulfilled

---

the work of Friedrich Gogarten, *Die Verkündigung Jesu Christi* (1948). As he says there, "If Jesus' death and resurrection are to be understood as his own death and resurrection, we must interpret them on the basis of his preaching. If that were not done, his death would be nothing but the failure of his mission, and the resurrection would be a nature miracle (*Mirakel*)" (pp. 147-148). The threat in this procedure for the way theology has traditionally worked is expressed by Ernst Käsemann when he observes that in the New Testament, even in the Gospel of John, the measure of right understanding is not the canon of the Bible but "recollection of the words of Jesus." (*Exegetische Versuche und Besinnungen*, Erster Band, Göttingen, 1960, p. 262.) These evidences of "a new quest of the historical Jesus" are enjoying the drama which transpires when students supercede their teacher, for it is at this point that the disciples of Bultmann believe they are going beyond him. Bultmann seems to have endorsed the position of the Gospel of John that when Jesus goes to his father in the resurrection, "the existence of his disciples is for the first time brought to fulfillment as an eschatological existence." (Rudolf Bultmann, *Das Evangelium des Johannes*, Göttingen, 1941, fifteenth edition, 1957, p. 386.) One ought not be so quick to conclude, however, that for Bultmann (and the Gospel of John) the gospel is of post-easter origin. When Jesus tells the disciples what to say about his resurrection he summarizes the message in one sentence: "I go to my father and your father, to my God and your God." But for Bultmann this is the author's way of saying that the Easter message includes "nothing basically different from what Jesus himself

in the resurrection: "I will not leave you orphans (ὀρφανούς)" (John 14:18). With God, the Father of Jesus, in the future, life of faith is an historical possibility. That is why "if Christ has not been raised our preaching is in vain and your faith is in vain" (1 Cor. 15:14).

The resurrection faith creates a people. An empty future inspires hopelessness, but the resurrection faith restores hope and becomes the condition for the creation of a new people. God's promise to Abraham to create a people is fulfilled in Jesus through whom a people is newly created. The resurrection faith, then, is the witness of the church that God is the one who has ordained Jesus, crucified by the world, to be Lord and Christ of the world. The old world of sin and death has come to an end in his sinless death and the new world of victory over sin and death has begun in his resur-

---

had already said to his followers" (p. 533). For that reason, furthermore, the Gospel of John criticizes the accent in the early church upon the resurrection appearances. These are considered at best as concessions to the weakness of the disciple Thomas, for "the word Jesus spoke" (John 2:22) should be enough to move one to faith (p. 539). When Jesus prepares his disciples for his death, he does not refer to the cross as a new offense but simply as a clarification of what the offense of Jesus really is, namely, "that a mere man whose life ends in death is the revealer of God" (p. 341). When Jesus washes the feet of the disciples, he is engaging in "a symbolic action" designed to interpret his ministry of obedience (p. 351, a theme in Bultmann which Fuchs now accentuates). "What applies to the exalted Christ also applies to the humiliated Christ. Even the historical form of Jesus, even his human history is included in the eschatological event through the hour of his glorification" (p. 377). The preaching of the church becomes a "repetition of (Jesus') preaching, that is, a recollection, as John 14:26 says" (p. 427). In a recent essay on the place of the historical Jesus in the interpretation of the Christian faith, Bultmann has made it clear that he is not averse to interpreting the Easter event in the light of the pre-easter history of Jesus. He simply warns that this historical emphasis could turn the historical Jesus into an object of historical research rather than into an object of faith. Nevertheless, he repeats his customary view about the Gospel of John: "One cannot project its claims back into the preaching of the historical Jesus." Thus he continues to resist what would seem to be implicit in his own historiographical understanding. That is, he re-

rection. Because of Christ's obedience to his mission in calling the world to obedience to God, in his cross he is himself dead to sin and alive to God, as are those who let his cross form their existence (Romans 6:9-11). In Paul's list of witnesses to the post-resurrection Lord he includes himself. By that he claims that the witness of the whole list has the same character as his own witness. He had seen Christians like Stephen win victory in death through their loyalty to Jesus of Nazareth. The God who is known as creator of the world through his vocation in Israel is now known as the one who has recreated the world, that is, "made it alive," through the vocation of Jesus of Nazareth.[23]

How does one give a witness to the occurrence of such an event? Not by standing in the structure of nature, for the facts of nature are not productive of the meanings of history. The knowledge of

---

fuses to find any continuity between the historical Jesus and the Christ of faith. (*Das Verhältnis der urchristlichen Christusbotschaft zum historischen Jesus*, Heidelberg, 1960, pp. 26 and 8, respectively.) Decisions such as these have had an effect upon Bultmann's understanding of the resurrection. "The Easter faith is the faith in the church as bearer of the *kerygma*" (*ibid.*, p. 27). This means that "there is no faith in Christ which is not at the same time faith in the church as the bearer of the *kerygma*, or, put in the terminology of dogmatics, faith in the Holy Spirit. But faith in the church is at the same time faith in Jesus Christ, which the historical Jesus has not demanded" (p. 26). The critics of Bultmann, therefore, do seem to have a case which bears importantly on how faith is to be conceived today. Bultmann has not required the definition of faith to be fully historicized. Instead, he encourages a rather traditional understanding of the Holy Spirit which augments historical work like a *deus ex machina*. If this were Shubert Ogden's reason for calling attention to Bultmann's lingering supernaturalism, rather than Bultmann's assertion of the uniqueness of Christ, which has a solid historiographical base, Ogden would be justified. (*See Christ Without Myth*, Harper, 1961.) James M. Robinson seems to be on firmer ground than Bultmann when he seeks to overcome the alleged chasm between the historical Jesus and the Christ of faith by the use of what he calls "modern historical method." (See *A New Quest of the Historical Jesus*, S.C.M. Press, London and Naperville, 1959.) The question then remains, What becomes of the now superfluous Holy Spirit? I have begun to speak

God and the formation of the Christian community cannot result from natural testimony. One witnesses to the resurrection historically, that is by expressing the meanings which the event revealed, by perpetuating "the voice" of the event which is its "message," for in that historical manner of speaking, the meanings occur again. That is the specific character of the rationality of history. The rationality of nature is a process of verification, establishing factuality and objectivity. Rationality in history is a process of understanding which knows that factuality and objectivity structure a reality which excludes man and thus, ironically, undercuts the expectation of meaningful existence. To mix these two forms of rationality therefore involves a painful irony. When nature attempts to embrace history, the structure of history evaporates. The effort to certify realities which are inherently meaningful forces into nature what belongs in history.

---

to this question within the framework of historiography rather than of traditional supernaturalism in the last section of this volume.

[23] Jean Héring's translation of Hebrews 11:17, 18 is most suggestive: " 'Through Isaac a posterity will be created (κληθήσεται=*suscitée*) for you.' For he considered that God is even able to raise (ἐγείρειν=*résusciter*) one from the dead." (*L'Epitre aux Hébreux*, Paris, 1954, pp. 106-08.) The allusion, presented in Hebrews as an Old Testament prefiguration of Christ's resurrection, makes resurrection a parallel of creation. In the same way the Apostle Paul relates creation to resurrection as new creation (2 Cor. 5:17). One ought not conclude from this that resurrection is interpreted by creation but rather that creation for the New Testament is interpreted by resurrection just as for the Old Testament creation was interpreted by the vocation of Israel. The Prologue to the Gospel of John is usually adduced as evidence of this (John 1:1-3). The baptismal liturgy of Colossians 1:15-20 also establishes Jesus of Nazareth as "the beginning" (ἀρχή), both because "in him all things were created" and because he is "the first-born from the dead." Baptism as "new creation" is "resurrection," as evidenced in the baptismal liturgy of Ephesians 5:14,

> Awake, O sleeper, and arise from the dead,
> And Christ shall give you light.

As Ernst Käsemann concludes, "There is no way to creation outside the

J. D. Salinger once had his little character, Teddy, say that "Logic was in the apple Adam ate. We must vomit it up if we are to learn to think clearly." This statement is only partially true, for there is more than one logic. There is a logic of nature and a logic of history. What was in the apple Adam ate was not logic but anxiety—the anxiety to have in nature what can only be true in history—the perverse anxiety to have the two things together which exist only in separation: the evidences of nature's logic and the inferences of history's logic. Historical understanding is born in the knowledge of this distinction and in the resolution to adopt the logic of history as the basis of one's life.

---

way through and in forgiveness." Another instructive instance has been pointed out by Käsemann. Ephesians 2:14-16 is a passage in which the doctrine of creation is said to be historicized in the light of the achievements of Christ. Just as in creation the chaos of the separation of heaven and earth was overcome by God's word so that a cosmos resulted, so in Christ God's word creates one new man where previously there were two. That is, according to Ephesians the "cosmic" conflict of Jew and Gentile is ended by reconciliation in the Church. (*Exegetische Versuche und Besinnungen,* Erster Band, pp. 51 and 280, respectively.)

CHAPTER 2

THE HISTORICAL FORM OF FAITH

Once the indissoluble link between life and thought in history has been effected, the doubts that have been expressed as to the *certainty* and the *utility* of history disappear altogether in a moment. How could that which is a *present* producing of our spirit ever be uncertain? How could that knowledge be *useless* which solves a problem that has come forth from the bosom of *life?*

BENEDETTO CROCE, *History: Its Theory and Practice,* Scholars' Classics, 1960, p. 15.

Faith should be built out of history.

MARTIN LUTHER, *Vorlesung über Jesaias,* Weimar Ausgabe, Vol. 31, Part 2, p. 242.

No one is asked to have faith in nature, because faith is impossible to structures which are external and objective, as nature is. For a quite different reason no one is asked to have faith in history, because history is meaning which illuminates and is not therefore offered for acceptance or rejection. If it illuminates, one lives it. If it does not illuminate, no amount of accepting will transform it into a faith. In nature man is a spectator and reality is a spectacle. If one "trusts" the universe of nature he does so in the brute sense in which he believes the sun will rise, or in the refined sense in which a science assumes the orderliness of nature. But one does not hold those convictions regarding nature in the same way he holds his loyalty to his country or his responsibility to his family. National and domestic events are history in a way that astral and marine events are not, for history is the structure of reality which supports our lives with meaning, events on the basis of which one lives significantly. The effete analogy from the scientist's faith in laws of nature to religious faith is utterly false in the light of this distinction. A Christian lives by his faith in God in a way in which a scientist does not live by his faith in the laws of nature. A man's faith is what infuses his life with the meanings which make his life negotiable. That cannot be said of the laws of science. A scientist may choose as the meaning of his life some such realization, developed through his work, that order is at the base of things or that the search for truth is man's primary vocation. That choice, however inferred from his occupation with the structure of nature, is itself an historical choice and not at all "scientific" in the sense which the term "scientific" enjoys in laboratory language. The reality in which man pursues his vocation as a scientist is history: being a scientist is meaningful work. The reality which the scientist structures in the pursuit of his vocation, however, is nature: raising the question of meaning is not laboratory procedure and even if it were would contribute nothing to the results of laboratory experiment.

Historical understanding unlike natural understanding is so similar to the way a man of faith understands as almost to be identical with it. Therefore, collision between faith and reason within the structure of history is reduced virtually to nothing. The mysteries of faith are in some sense only as mysterious as the mysteries of history. The methods by which we know our faith are in some ways identical to the methods by which we know anything else historical. These claims, of course, place a heavier burden on the expositor than has as yet been assumed. One ought to define more extensively what history is and how the character of history informs the methods by which it is known. When that has been done, it should be clearer why one can say that the form of historical understanding is in some sense also the structure of faith.

I. THE MATERIALITY OF THE HISTORICAL WORLD

History is the structure of reality in which the question of meaning is raised. He only walks in history who walks where the authenticity of human existence is at issue. History is the reality which has to do with our life in so far as its essential humanness is involved. By this definition, a great number of concerns which often classify as history, do not really belong. The most persistent of this sort is the question, "Did it really happen?" The question of the existence of something in history is not yet an historical question until it is also the question of human existence there.[1] The word "existence"

[1] "The brute fact of the assassination (of Caesar) interests no one if it is not put in its place in the totality constituted by the crisis of the Roman Republic, the resistance of the senatorial aristocracy to personal power, etc." (Raymond Aron, *Dimensions de la conscience historique*, Paris, 1961, p. 52.) "We already knew the biography of Robespierre . . . as a succession of well-established facts. These facts appear concrete because they are known in detail but they lack *reality* since we can no longer connect them to the totalizing movement." (Jean-Paul Sartre, *Critique de la raison dialectique*, Vol. I, Paris, 1960, p. 86.) "Actual historians are the descendants of chroniclers and annalists, whose job it was to make the calendars for the popes. But later the historian confined himself to noting conspicuous facts:

is being used equivocally in modern speech wherever one does not distinguish between existence as factuality and existence as justifiability, importance, or authenticity. The question about factuality, being a question of nature, has nothing in common with the question about authenticity, which is the properly historical question. To be sure, there is some fact for every meaning, but the meaning never derives its validity from the fact. The fact is never the cause of the meaning. A statement of fact may help to *settle* an historical question but it is not itself an historical statement. The question of fact, being posed from the outside, forecloses on the possibility of meaning, which is a participation inwardly. History is a realm in which meanings are at stake, and meanings are never given as facts.

Is this reasoning an open door to unbridled subjectivism and unanchored meanings? Must the ideas of history float in air? Does this kind of historical thinking sponsor a form of angelism or Platonism? On the contrary, the big deception in some historical circles is to assume that facts anchor meaning, whereas it is meanings which give to facts whatever duration they enjoy. As Pirandello has said, "A fact, like a sack, cannot stand up unless it is filled." Voltaire, the first scientific historian in the modern sense, was probably the first modern to realize the hegemony of meaning

---

facta et dicta memorabilia. These facts struck the imagination by their strangeness or merited being narrated by reason of the quality of the persons they concerned. In this epoch, history really only studied the facts, retaining the most notable. We continue to speak the same language, but the usage has become improper since history concerns itself less with describing than with interpreting. When it will once again have more clearly realized its function, the expression 'historical facts' will rejoin the forgotten quantity of other usages which have not been able to adapt themselves to the new needs of the science." (H. Lévy-Bruhl, "Une Notion confusée: le fait historique," in *Recherches Philosophiques*, Vol. V, Paris, 1935-36, pp. 273, 274.) For the canons of historical criticism, preoccupation with factual details, such as whether the demoniac was an only son, or which of the servant's ears was amputated by Peter, and whether the name of the victim was Malchus, is a sign not of greater but of lesser historical validity.

over fact. That realization affected his writing of history. Factuality was subordinated and the human reality of history was allowed to emerge. Theologians are just beginning to profit by the implications in that historical procedure. The advance for the Christian faith is the role which history as a meaningful reality plays in the connotation of the rationality of faith.

The world of meaning is a structure with a very definite shape. It is neither a world of purely personal consciousness, populated by thinking things, nor a world of impersonal objects, imporous to thought. It is an interworld defined by the mutual interpenetration of subjects and objects. The world of meaning is constructed out of the mutual participation of subjective sentiment for meaning and objective sedimentation of meaning. Historical subjectivity is the personal passion for a life of meaning. Historical objectivity is the trace of meaning left by other subjects. Where the constancy of the historical object merges with the intentionality of the historical subject, history is formed. The essence of that formation is meaning, a reality neither subjective nor objective because existing as an interworld, a world between, a world being called in contemporary philosophy a *Lebenswelt*, a specifically human world. It is a world in which there are no objects but only objects-for-subjects, and a world in which there are no subjects, but only subjects-for-objects.

Historical understanding is a process which occurs in this human world of intersubjectivity. The process consists in what every professional historian does when he pursues his craft sensitively. What is even more striking, it consists in what every man does when he conducts his life authentically. The private consciousness is set within a public world. History, objectively viewed, is the sedimentation of meanings left by the public world. History, subjectively viewed, is the process of recovering the meanings which continue to make a world possible. The recoverability of meanings is based on two possibilities: first, that what is there was once meaningful; second, that living men are drawn to meanings, because meaning is what they seek. Hence, there are two conditions for the possibility of historical understanding. One is that I am myself an historical being, interested in forming a meaningful world on the basis of a world of meanings. The other is that I exist in a community of historical beings which leaves the traces of its life as a map for future life.

Because history is meaning and not fact, the test of the authenticity of an historian is his capacity to emerge in his culture as a violent man, a kind of prophet who tears the outer garments from events to expose their tender contours. Historical understanding will usually appear as the knowledge of something previously hidden. Yet when that knowledge is made available, it does not need promotion from agencies of influence and power, for it strikes the ear of man with a ring of rightness. The Frenchman, Montaigne, once told about three savages who observed men bowing before the infant king, Charles IX, and they could see no reason why. Pascal commented that those savages lacked the understanding of a reason hidden in an apparent folly, namely that the orderliness of a state is best conserved by the practice of installing as ruler the first-born son of the king. Whether he be child or beast, there will always be a king, a necessity for civil peace.

The understanding of historical events is not available to eyewitnesses but only to historians, who by acts of interpretation can penetrate beneath what eyes behold, to the meanings buried there. The capacity of those meanings to survive as history is not determined by the historian, for it depends mainly upon two things: first, inherent authenticity, which is not an attribute of its simply having occurred, having been observed and recorded; second, the historical finesse of a people in recalling the event in the terms which give it its original meaningfulness. Wherever either of these conditions is lacking, events cease being history. Historical events like the drama cannot survive the absence of an appreciative audience.

The Old Testament records a story which admirably illustrates the historical problem. God arranged that the people who beheld the bronze serpent Moses made would be saved from the mortal effects of snake bite (Numbers 21). When the people looked at the bronze serpent, therefore, they did not look at what Moses had made but at what God had promised. That is the role of the historical understanding—to penetrate beneath the artifacts of culture for the fundamental meaning which justifies their endurance as history. But there is a danger in the procedure. In the case of Moses' bronze serpent, the people gradually failed to see it as the promise of God. Making it an object in itself, they burned incense to it. King Hezekiah simply accelerated the erosion which history would inevitably have effected when he ordered the serpent destroyed. Historical events are idolatrous when they are remembered without being understood, and idolatry is the death of history.

The interests of historical rationality are identical with the interests of a prophetic faith. The world of faith is a world of meaning which is supported by the occurrence of events whose validity is not extrinsic. The eyes of faith are not the eyes of fact-finders but of prophets and apostles—interpreters—who "see" what these events are really about. Faith declines when the meanings which distinguish the events are supplanted or coated over with concerns unrelated to their original historical power. In the New Testament an eyewitness is not a fact-finder but an interpreter. Marcel Proust said, "We do not see until we have understood." That sequence is true alike for faith and history. Errors of interpretation which arise out of failure to understand the meaning of "eyewitnesses" in the New Testament are crucial. Jesus had that error to contend with. He once made the statement to his contemporaries, "Your father Abraham rejoiced that he was to *see* my day; he *saw* it and was glad" (John 8:56). The crowd responded, "You are not yet fifty years old and have you *seen* Abraham?" So they attempted to stone him. "Sight" for Jesus, however, was not an ocular but an interpretive phenomenon. The New Testament materials suffer at the hands of interpreters who assume that references to "eyewitnesses" and "appearances" are optical allusions.

Origen, the first systematic theologian, had sound historiographical instincts when he elaborated the ambiguity involved in beholding Jesus:

> Not everyone who saw Christ when he was here in the flesh could see him as he really was. His Disciples could—they could see how great he was, they could see he was divine. That, it seems to me, explains the Saviour's reply to Philip's request: 'Lord, let us see the Father' (John xiv. 8). That is why he said: 'Anyone who has seen me, Philip, has seen the Father' (cf. John xiv. 9). Pilate too saw Jesus, but the Jesus he saw was not the real one. And Judas the traitor never saw he was the Christ.[2]

The task of the theologian, like the task of the historian, is to stir up the sentiment of meaning in the sedimentation of events, and not to celebrate the sedimentation. For those who think man lives by facts, the pursuit of meaning will appear as a form of historical violence. The classic rebuff which organized Christians direct at the more violent among their interpreters has been, "They have taken away my Lord and I know not where they have laid him." The pathos of this scene is that the fact-finders are bidding to supplant the historians. The eye which sees without understanding beholds only the shell which the living organism has secreted. The task of the historian is to discern the living organism. He is motivated by the passion of the prophet, "Oh that I knew where I might find him," and he will heed the warning of the angels at the tomb of the resurrected Lord, "Why seek ye the living among the dead?"

History, then, is not a description of events occurring on the surface of a world not history. History *is* a world, a *Lebenswelt*, a

[2] *Homily on Luke*, 3. See also *Against Celsus* 6, 77; *Commentary on Matthew* 12, 36. Quoted by Jean Daniélou, *Origen*, trans. by Walter Mitchell, Sheed and Ward, 1955, p. 260. Cf. "The emphasis is not upon the act of seeing as such but upon the revelatory character of the events", in Hans Frhr. von Campenhausen, *Der Ablauf der Ostereignisse und das leere Grab*, second edition, Heidelberg, 1958, p. 9, note 5. Cf. also Ernst Käsemann, *Exegetische Versuche und Besinnungen*, Vol. I, Göttingen, 1960, pp. 249, 250.

world of its own, the world it shapes. This world is not a neutral field existing outside men. It is the field of force they help comprise. Man is in this world, not alongside it. He is in it not as something to which he belongs but as something which belongs to him and for which he is responsible. History becomes a world only through the mediation of man. Man is with this world as a family is with its home—not inserted into it as from the outside, as a coin in a box, but integral to it, enmeshed in it, living by it as it lives by him.

An understanding of the human world helps to demonstrate why the object of historical life is different from objects of nature and, likewise, why the subject is different from the naked self of the Cartesian *cogito*. The world of history is an interworld of subjects-which-are-objects and objects-which-are-subjects, where the conditions for a complete life prevail. There man is not a being who is added to nature. He is the creator of a different species of world, no part of which is comprehensible apart from him. It is the kind of world John Betjeman intimates when he sings of his boyhood in *Summoned by Bells*,

> Safe, in a world of trains and buttered toast
> Where things inanimate could feel and think.

Betjeman subsequently retreats a bit from the human world when he professes to prefer the world of "slate and granite mothered by centuries of sea" to the world of "polished wood and stone tortured by Father's craftsmen into shapes." He was in revolt against the human world because it was the world of his Father, who tried to kill the poet in him. The Russian poet Pasternak showed a more muscular ability to survive a hostile history when he asserted,

> I squeeze a world in stanzas.

Modern artists like Cézanne in his cubist phase have contributed to the comprehension of the human world in a negative way. In picturing the world abstractly, they have shown it as it would be if there were no man in it, thus no history. It is a world of landscapes without wind, water without movement, objects frozen in place as at the origin of things before man appeared—a strange world, without familiarity, resisting all overtures of human communion. It is not, as one commonly supposes, a solidly reliable world existing of necessity and always there. That supposition is suspended when abstraction shows the world alienated from its fundamental humanness, without a history.[3]

The novels of the French anti-novelist, Alain Robbe-Grillet, may come to have the same negative effect on the understanding of history as abstract art has had. With their deliberate expurgation of anything specifically human from the story of man's life, they are an artistic conspiracy which leaves the reader gaping at a landscape so sanitary it is uninhabitable by living men. In his novel, *Jalousie,* he describes a woman reclining on her bed as if she were a chance collocation of geometrical angles and dimensions. He describes a "living room" as if he were a housebreaker casing the place. The activities of his "human" characters are forced throughout to share the stage on equal footing with a lizard and a centipede. Jealousy is an emotion described in this novel in such a way that it could easily be confused with the jalousies which cut the sunlight into horizontal lines behind the window. In short, these novels of Robbe-Grillet are like abstract art. If projected on a screen, they

[3] I have been instructed here by the analysis of Cézanne made by Maurice Merleau-Ponty, *Sens et Non-Sens,* Paris, 1948, pp. 18-44. Paul Tillich, by drawing quite a different conclusion about Cézanne, reveals a certain lack of seriousness with history. He describes the work of Cézanne as revealing "in this very unorganic form . . . the power of being itself," a disruptedness which "is nothing else than an attempt to look into the depths of reality, below any surface." (*Christianity and the Existentialists,* edited by Carl Michalson, Scribners, 1958, pp. 136, 137.) Tillich wrongly characterizes this method as the existentialist level of modern art, for existential structures do not reveal being but only openness, only possibility. Ontological philosophies like Tillich's have in common with traditional theologies the questionable supposition that the meanings man lives by will be derivatives of something transcending history which is more significant than history.

would resemble radar more than cinema. This particular novel, written with dry mouth and blank stare, is the account by a jealous husband of every movement of his wife with another man. There is a madness in his prose, a hatred for the world, which, like jealousy, punishes life by eliminating all human feeling from the things one sees, or punishes the observer by enforcing a fast from the meanings of the human world, dwelling on the minute and insignificant detail. If a historian were to describe the world in this voyeuristic style or a theologian to express his faith in this hermitic, self-flagellatory spirit one would say of him he is surely a man sterilized by disappointment or hate or some other instrument of meaninglessness.[4]

While this kind of evaluation is not as easy to make regarding "the new music," it is very tempting. One hesitates to make statements about new forms of art. The new enjoys the luxury of a period of unsteady acceptance which feeds on man's hope that something ever more authentic is emerging. One would like to think, for instance, that the music of Bela Bartók, like the abstract art of painting and novel, had discerned aesthetic forms which permit a new dimension of vision and sound to emerge. Abstract art has been likened to religious movements whose founders withdrew to the desert or the wilderness prior to forming the world. There is a world of difference, however, between monasticism as flight from the world and monasticism as a method of shaping the world. Some modern art-forms now enjoy the luxury of not being identifiable as flight yet not having demonstrated that they are shaping the world. A British critic recently said, "Bartók concerts

[4] The novels of Albert Camus could be considered forerunners to this socalled anti-novel movement represented by Robbe-Grillet. In *The Stranger*, the most passionate events are viewed as from the outside, "a purely objective recital." *The Plague* is a history of the effect of an epidemic upon a city, and Camus chooses for his "historian" a medical doctor who admits one cannot heal and think at the same time. The whole method of detachment could have begun in Stendhal's *Charterhouse of Parma* where Fabrice races back and forth across Napoleon's battlefield making observations which are utterly unrelated to the world-shaking meaning of Waterloo.

make me itch." The ambiguity in that sensation is that one cannot tell by it whether he is allergic to Bartók or whether he is reliving through the music the mood of restlessness and irritation which the composer felt when writing. Artists, like theologians, run the risk of employing forms which are permissible in nature but which are alien to history, like certain frequencies audible to animal ears which remain unheard by men. Not that the "new music" is sub-human. It is simply that the genius of what is done may be not so much to have admitted man to a new dimension of sound as to have shown man how a world sounds when he as man is being rejected. Aaron Copland once said there are five moods in music: blues, romantic, lyric, decadence, and protest. One might classify the new music as protest which, by Copland's definition, is "an angry, sometimes vicious attack on life." After all, medieval theorists called the augmented fourth, so essential in the new music, *diabolus in musica.* A newspaper cartoon following the first audition of Strauss' *Electra* depicted the composer as an executioner. After the playing of Copland's own First Symphony, the conductor, Walter Damrosch, turned to the enthusiastic audience and said, "If a young man at the age of twenty-three can write a symphony like that, in five years he will be ready to commit murder."

Modern art at least fulfills a significant historical role. Modern science, by contrast, is not historical—neither in form nor in intention. It conceives a world which is exclusive of the eminently human world. This is not its weakness but its strength—its vocation. Anyone who attempts to lure it into another occupation is asking it to be something other than natural science. Modern art, however, is historical in intention although not in form. It conceives a world which cannot be called exclusive of man because it stands over against man aggressively, engaging man as the structure of nature does not. Nature stands parallel to history; art stands in dispute with history. Art in its modern phase is not historical in form because like nature it has not positively embraced man in his full humanity. It is historical in intention possibly because, unlike nature, it is designed to arouse in man an historical consciousness by showing him how it feels to be excluded.

History, which is a world of meaning, is a world of objects, but they are objects vital with the human intention, and not geometrical, empty, bloodless or inert, victims of forces outside them. They are bodies of which it can be said they are *in* the world, because in fact they live the world. They are in the world as the heart is in the organism.[5] While the objects of history exist side by side they do not relate after the fashion of a book's relation to a table. They relate as hands side by side—capable of the same kind of corporeal displacement and subject to the same kind of chemical reduction as any other bodies, yet phenomena of a completely different order and requiring a completely different method of analysis. The objects of the human world are there more like works of art than like physical objects, organized complexly from the inside with a human intention toward the outside. The objects of the human world, like hands side by side, are interiorly tense with voluntary springs, mysterious to decipher, contributing to the exhilaration of life in direct proportion to their profundity, yet blocking clear and exact perception in that same proportion. Being not simply objects but objects charged with meaning, they belong not to the natural cosmos but to what Count von Yorck astutely labelled the "historical cosmos," the *Lebenswelt.*[6] One assumes it was this aspect of history which the French historian Michelet had in mind when he said, "I move across history like the Greek actress who, when playing Electra, bore the funeral urn of her own son."[7]

History as a world of meaning, therefore, is nonetheless a world.

[5] Merleau-Ponty's analogy, *Phénoménologie de la Perception*, Paris, 1945, p. 235.

[6] Fritz Kaufmann, "Die Philosophie des Grafen Paul Yorck von Wartenberg," *Jahrbuch für Philosophie und phänomenologische Forschung*, 1928, Vol. IX, p. 46.

[7] *Ma Jeunesse*, Paris, 1884, p. xvi.

It has a materiality, an externality, an *extra nos* character. But its exteriority is defined by its interiority; the shape and weight of its massiveness is controlled by its meaning. The outsideness of a reality when approached from its exteriority is not the same as the outsideness of a reality when approached from its interiority. Hegel has stated the situation with startling lucidity. In his *Phenomenology of Mind* he has said, "Organic nature has no history."[8] The reason for that distinction is that "the whole is not present in it; and the whole is not there because the whole is not as such there for itself." The meaning of this statement is prepared for step by step. First, in historical thinking the question of empirical existence is put in parentheses or, as the contemporary phenomenologists say, "bracketed out." These empirical qualities are indispensable to things in themselves, but the consciousness can dispense with them.[9] Second, history is that alone which concerns "manifestations" or "appearances," that is, that which is available to the consciousness. "What does not appear is nothing for consciousness at all."[10] Finally, does this not confirm the widespread suspicion about Hegel, the suspicion which Marx and Kierkegaard popularized, that Hegel lived and thought in terms of a disembodied spirit? Not at all. Hegel simply knew the difference between the historical cosmos and the natural cosmos. The natural cosmos is an exterior reality which has no interior reality. The historical cosmos, having an interior reality, also has an exterior reality, but an exterior which is different from other exteriorities. As Hegel says, "The aspect which is called 'inner' has its own 'outer' aspect, which is distinct from what is in general called the outer."[11]

[8] J. B. Baillie edition, p. 326.

[9] *Ibid*, p. 286. In his massive history called *The Phenomenological Movement* H. Spiegelberg is probably not wrong to observe that the Hegelian phenomenology never practiced "the bracketing operation, certainly not explicitly." But it is clear that Hegel knew about it. Vol. I, The Hague, 1960, p. 7.

[10] J. B. Baillie edition, *op. cit.*, p. 289.

[11] *Ibid.*, p. 303.

This particular discussion of Hegel's is usually overlooked, for the remarkable reason that it is located in his lengthy attack on phrenology, a faddist movement of his time. A phrenologist is one who thinks he can tell what is inside a head by studying the outside of the head. Judged by that criterion, phrenology is not a fad which died but a cultural habit which persists. A phenomenology of spirit is the alternative to a phrenology of spirit. It is not a repudiation of the reality of externals. It is a repudiation of methods which seek internals by way of externals, and an endorsement of methods which seek externals by way of internals. An historian can learn something of this phenomenological lesson from the novelist who writes about the discomforts of a leper colony without mentioning physical pain, in order to let the attention be drawn to the suffering.

The thing which has no interiority is called by Hegel *Ding* or *Sache* and is translated into French by Jean Hyppolite as *la chose,* into English by J. B. Baillie as "matter of fact." The thing which has interiority, the historical thing, is called by Hegel *die Sache selbst* and translated as *La Chose* and "fact of the matter" or "real intention." History as a meaningful reality, far from being a realm of subjectivity, is known to Hegel as "the higher objectivity." To treat history as a "matter of fact" is what the Germans call *Historie.* To treat it in terms of its "real intention" is what they call *Geschichte.* With no intention of detracting from the monumental English translation of Heidegger's *Sein und Zeit,* one may deplore that this rich philological background for Heidegger's work is not conserved in the translation of these terms. *Sache* is indifferently called "thing," "matter" or "affair," while *die Sachen selbst* is rendered as "the things themselves," throwing upon the reader a very heavy burden of interpretation.

In his later thought, Martin Heidegger has attributed to *das Ding* the characteristics of Hegel's *die Sache selbst.* He has done so by analyzing a thing as a complex of four dimensions—earth, sky, mortals, and gods, calling it a foursome or a square. The thing therefore has the capacity to organize men's life into a world. As such, however, it can no longer be called *Historie* or nature. It is *Geschichte*. Hence it cannot perform, as the Swiss theologian Heinrich Ott has recently proposed that it can, as a way beyond the duality of nature and history. It simply reinforces the relevance of the duality. Long before Heidegger attributed these historical characteristics to "the thing," Rudolf Bultmann had shown how "body" in Pauline thinking was a notion primarily historical.[12]

Christians who wish to stress the objectivity of their faith often allow themselves to be tricked into expressing it in the categories of *Historie*, which is really to naturalize history. Even the Bible is not immune to this strategy. As Ernst Käsemann has warned,

> To hold fast to *Historie* is one way in which the *extra nos* of salvation finds its expression. How risky this way really is can be illustrated from the Gospel of Luke, since there the author turns the *kairos* into an epoch, predestination into a continuous development, the granting of salvation prior to our faith into the finding of demonstrable facts prior to our acknowledgement, grace into our destiny which requires everyone to decide between belief and unbelief, the righteousness of the church into the organization of the Christian religion.[13]

The irony of this passion for securing the interiority of faith by attaching it to some exteriority has been explored in a very novel way by Friedrich Gogarten. He has shown how, in attempting to secure its objectivity, one may overlook the intrinsic intelligibility of the faith and supply a standard of intelligibility of his own choosing. That is why the claim to objectivism is, ironically, a form of subjectivism.[14] For fear of subjectivism in an historical

[12] For a discussion of Heidegger, Ott, and Bultmann on this issue see the book edited by James Robinson and John Cobb, *The Later Heidegger and Theology*, Harper, 1963, especially the introductory essay by Robinson.

[13] *Exegetische Versuche und Besinnungen*, Vol. I, p. 202.

[14] See his *The Reality of Faith*, The Problem of Subjectivism in Theology, translated by Carl Michalson and others, Westminster, 1959. As Peep says in Ionesco's play, *The Killer*, "Objectivity is subjective in the para-scientific

faith one adopts an objectivity which not only misses the higher objectivity of the faith but ends as a form of subjectivism.

In his discussion of the higher objectivity of faith Hegel anticipated Gabriel Marcel's distinction between "being" and "having." The reason, for which things are simply there as facts for an observer, Hegel called the "having" reason. The reason, for which things are intentions concerned with one's *self*-consciousness, he called the "being" reason. Karl Marx is also anticipated in this distinction, for these two kinds of reason separate two types of people, the citizens of "daily" intelligence for whom society is something simply there "in itself," and the revolutionary for whom society is there "for him," as his responsibility.[15] Martin Heidegger was later to characterize the "having" reason as the impersonal "daily one" whose life is all curiosity and gossip, thus simply "being there." The "being" reason, on the other hand, "ex-ists," that is, transcends itself, moving beyond banal history to an authentic history of responsibility.

Some may fear that this penchant for dividing people into two groups, the common, banal group who hold the object of their faith as from the outside, and the spiritually quick, self-conscious group, who hold their faith by way of its interior meaning, if applied to the Christian community, would reinstate the old gnostic

---

age." Cf. James M. Robinson's excellent statement in *A New Quest of the Historical Jesus*, S.C.M. Press, London, 1959 (published in the U.S.A. by Alec R. Allenson, Inc.), p. 96, n. 1:

> Twentieth-century historiography need not surrender the term 'objective' to nineteenth-century historiography. Scholarly objectivity does not reside simply in classifying the particular in categories with wider acceptance than one's own individual view, for such a procedure is blind to the two-fold subjectivity residing in the categories of one's school of thought or day and age, and in the pervasive subjectivity of Western rationalism, which blunts true encounter into a merely outward stimulus for one's inner *a priori* faculties. Instead, objectivity resides in a complete openness to what the creative historical event has to say. This involves a willingness to listen for underlying intentions and the understanding of existence they convey, with an ear sharpened by one's own awareness of

hierarchy between the ordinary Christian who lives by blind belief and the illuminated Christian who knows what he believes. Quite candidly, a comprehension of the faith as an historical reality destroys this method of distinguishing Christians in two groups, for it raises the question even more radically. Is one really in any sense "in faith" except as his life is embraced "gnostically," that is, meaningfully? If that be Gnosticism, the historical consciousness today confers on the work of the early Christian "gnostics," Origen and Clement of Alexandria, a relevance it did not achieve in their time. To be a Christian is to enjoy, to live by, to possess a self-consciousness of faith and to be illuminated by that faith. Christian faith is synonymous with meaning, that is, with an historical reason whose search for meaningful existence finds its corollary in the meaningful event of God's activity in Jesus of Nazareth.

II. THE RATIONALITY OF THE HISTORICAL WORLD

A. THE METHOD OF HISTORICAL UNDERSTANDING

If history is a world of meaning and Christianity is an historical faith, the implications for the rationality of the faith are evident. Four dominant elements can be specified which constitute the form of historical understanding and are operative, therefore, in the rationality of faith.

a. In faith as in history nothing will be known apart from some

---

the problems of human existence, and a willingness to suspend one's own answers and one's own understanding of existence sufficiently to grasp as a real possibility what the other is saying. Thus one's historical involvement, not one's disinterestedness, is the instrument leading to objectivity, and it must be constantly observed that this 'subjective participation' of the historian consists precisely in the potential suspension of his own personal views, for the sake of hearing what the other has to tell him about his existence.

[15] *Phenomenology of Spirit*, Hoffmeister edition, pp. 252 and 315; Baillie edition, pp. 370 and 459f.

prior interest in knowing. History remains dumb apart from an interlocutor. The secrets of history remain all locked up apart from an aggressive historical curiosity. The womb of history remains undelivered apart from the obstetric force of human interest. "The question and the selection of the question is the first step in historical research."[16] In Biblical literature the role of the interested human question is utterly decisive for faith. One may shake history to the foundations by the nocturnal whisper, "What must I do to be saved?" Yet one may just as easily seal himself off from meaningful history by the clinical inquiry, "Where are you from?" The mission of Jesus was blocked wherever he was confronted by such questions as "Where are you from?", for they revealed fundamental disinterestedness. History, like Christ before Pilate, remains silent in the presence of questions which do not draw upon meaning. Lack of interest is not primarily an attribute of carelessness but of lack of care. According to Sophocles' *Philoctetes,* Odysseus once asked Neoptolemus, "You clearly recollect all I have told you?" And the reply was given, "Yes, now that I have understood it." The French novelist, Stendhal, spoke with a sure feeling for the rationality of history when he said in his Journal, "I have an absolute lack of memory for what does not interest me."[17] The questions which give one access to historical understanding are not the questions that are already so full of a certain kind of wisdom that they thwart the arrival of new understanding. The fertile historical question emanates from a knowledge simply of what one does not know but knows he must know. Karl

[16] Johann Gustav Droysen, *Historik,* edited by Rudolf Hübner, second edition, Munich and Berlin, 1943, p. 36.

[17] Cited by Georges Gusdorf, *Mémoire et Personne,* Vol. I, Paris, 1951, p. 246. Charles Hartshorne, professional philosopher and amateur ornithologist, has observed that birds with complicated, interesting songs sing almost without interruption, while birds with uninteresting songs "are quiet about 70 per cent of the time. . . . The simple-song bird has a short span of attention and 'forgets' his song during the pause." From Prof. Hartshorne's address to the American Ornithological Association, as reported in the *New York Times,* Sept. 12, 1954.

Barth once cautioned preachers that "the people want an answer to the question, 'Is it true?' "[18] Perhaps, rather, like Dostoevsky's Ivan, they want the answer to *their questions*. The human question is not "Is it true?" but "Is it meaningful?" Man by himself is that kind of question needing an answer, that kind of emptiness waiting to be filled.[19] Answering a genuinely human question is not so much like filling a void as like keeping a promise.

b. In faith as in history nothing will be known apart from some prior manifestation of knowledge. Acts of historical understanding are dependent upon significant historical events which quicken and inform. One of the most conspicuous developments in the history of historical method is the effect the French Revolution had upon the eighteenth- and nineteenth-century historians' interest in history. Once having experienced an earthquake, one is sensitive to the imminence of earthquakes. History reveals its meanings with apocalyptic suddenness, before one even asks or thinks, and by those revelations lifts one's thinking to new levels of understanding. Students who are forced by academic exigency to mine through historical tomes for data that seem to lie there inert ought not be allowed to forget that those craters were once formed by fire. The sense of the priority of tongues of fire in the backgrounds of *sacred* literature is no different in its relevance to historical discernment. Theological and historical literature have this priority of the revealing event in common with tragic literature. Sighs of sympathy are not simply subjective expressions, for they are aroused by scenes of wretchedness. Shudders of fear are not simply interior states, for they are evoked by chilling episodes. The historian, Dilthey, therefore, was justified in rejecting introspection as a method of historical understanding. In questions of meaning one does not examine his subjective states for answers. He examines himself in his relation to the objective realities which

[18] *The Word of God and the Word of Man*, translated by Douglas Horton, Zondervan, 1935, p. 115.

[19] Adopted from Hamann, as cited by R. Gregor Smith, *J. G. Hamann: A Study in Christian Existentialism*, Harper, 1960, p. 48.

produced those states. Every object to be historical implicates a subject. Every subject to be historical indicates an object.

c. In faith as in history nothing will be known apart from an act of interpretation. Interpretation is the act in which the historian negotiates between his sentiment for historical meaning and the sedimentation of meaning which encounters his sentiment. This interdependence of sentiment and sediment in acts of interpretation is what is known today as "the hermeneutical circle." How does one negotiate between two priorities, the prior question about meaning and the prior manifestation of meaning? In the same fashion as one negotiates between fetal realities and obstetric instruments. While there are no historical answers without historical questions, the questions do not engender the answers; the answers satisfy the questions. Historical understanding will not create a multiplicity of private worlds of meaning as long as it is known that the constants of history are available in the sedimentation. In the act of interrogation by the historical sentiment, the private perspective is surrendered along with other forms of prejudgment, and the valid private concern is embraced by what is there in history for all.

The Spanish philosopher, Ortega, once conjured up the situation of a great man dying. At his side were his wife, his doctor, a journalist and an artist. Which of the four grasps the situation most accurately? The wife is too biased by emotional proximity. The journalist is too biased by the political stance of his newspaper. The doctor is too biased by anxiety over his reputation as a healer. The artist is too biased by his "purely perceptive attitude," being "directed exclusively toward the visual part." Considering the emotional proximity of the wife and the emotional distance of the artist, "it seems doubtful whether the two can be said to be present at the same event." But as to which of the four points of view captures the meaning of the situation, Ortega concludes that "the answer, no matter how we decide, cannot but be arbitrary. Any preference can be founded on caprice only."[20]

[20] *The Dehumanization of Art*, Doubleday Anchor Book, 1956, p. 14.

While this brief discussion is carried on under the title of " A Few Drops of Phenomenology," Ortega underestimated the passionate neutrality of historical procedures. A phenomenology of history brackets out the biases which interpose artificial distances between an interpreter and his data. In that sense it is neutral. But it also enters into the concerns which constitute events as humanly meaningful. In that sense it is passionate. Acts of historical interpretation combine the emotional proximity of love with the emotional distance of art. Thus they conserve meanings which evaporate and erode when entrusted to a care which is either too tender or too abstract.

Henry James is known to have taken a vague and second-hand story from an Archbishop of Canterbury and built it into a novel. In doing so he confirmed the theory of Thomas Wolfe that a novel is not fiction but fact interpreted. But history, unlike the novel, is not fact interpreted. Historians and theologians are not at liberty to take fragments of the past and to fold them into the process of their present interests. Interpretation is thus distinguishable from interpolation. For history is the act of interpreting something which has no status as a fact apart from the structure of interpretation. In a very minimum of terms Sartre has described this act in which the historian goes out of himself to seize his data interpretively: "Interiority exteriorizes itself in order to interiorize the exteriority."[21]

d. In faith as in history nothing will be known apart from a risk of judgment. Exactitude and correctness inspire the methods of nature but are unrealizable in history. If history were geometry or geography, there would be no risks. But history originates in the ambiguity of decision, in the passion of human dialogue, in collusion between parties, in the collision of contradictory impulses each emanating from opaque depths, in the collective human drive for the construction of a significant world, in acts of freedom which are so original that nothing prior to them explains

[21] *Critique de la raison dialectique*, Vol. I, Paris, 1960, p. 149.

them. The historical structure of reality cannot be fixed in phrases which correspond mathematically to things as they are. If historians were to follow the Cartesian injunction to accept nothing that cannot be doubted, the range of their literature would shrink to banalities which lack the power to inform the future. Yet, because meaningful life waits upon historical judgments, these judgments must be made despite the risks. The situation of Jesus of Nazareth pressed by Judaism to decide whether he is the Christ is more like the situation of Louis XVI at the fall of the Bastille than of Isaac Newton at the fall of the apple. In nature, problems are posed and the universe patiently awaits a resolution which can ultimately be made with clarity and distinctness. In history, problematical situations arise which couple urgency with ambiguity. If historical understanding is just to the quality of history, it will know its data in the very atmosphere of courage in which history itself was born. Jesus himself had no mathematical certainty of his messiahship. That lack of certainty was no barrier to his complete obedience to God. If faith is just to the historical context in which it arises, a Christian will not require his own obedience to God to be held in suspense to a test of certainty which Jesus did not even require of himself.

Data from the structure of nature are given in the mode of certainty, yet lack the qualities which contribute to the fundamental needs of human life. Data from the structure of history are precisely the answers to human needs, yet they lack certainty. Considering that situation, the desire for certainty is like a magic skin, a talisman which we hold in our hand. Every time we invoke the wish for certainty we can feel the skin shrink; and, like the magic skin in Balzac's story, when the skin is gone, our significant life will be ended. There is an urgency regarding uncertain meanings, as contrasted with a lack of urgency regarding things which are certain. Isaac Newton did not rush into print with his remarkable scientific discoveries. They were published so long after he made them that others, who made and published the same discoveries much later, could nevertheless charge Newton with plagiarism.

The note of urgency in scientific work at mid-twentieth century is not intrinsic to the structure of nature with which science is concerned. It is intrinsic to the structure of history, that is, to the political situation which is constantly making science its handmaiden. It is true, of course, that Newton was as phlegmatic with respect to his theological and historical writings as with respect to his scientific works. That may be accounted for when it is realized that his theological writings were virtually as oriented to nature as were his scientific writings.

Traditionally, historical interpretation was made in three successive stages: understanding, exegesis and application. In contemporary hermeneutics, understanding and exegesis are merged. One does not first understand, then explain. The understanding must be self-explaining. Thereafter, what becomes of the responsibility for applying what is understood? If historical understanding is an act of decisiveness, meaning ought not be looked upon as an intellectual preface to action. Meaning is itself a kind of action; meaning is realized in action. Theologians endorse this method of interpretation when they refuse to separate theology and ethics: faith *is* what a man does that is meaningful. Revivalism denies the method when preachers add appeals for decision to their interpretation of the faith. Faith is *not* what a man does *with* the claims of the gospel. Faith is the act of being claimed by the gospel in such a way as to have one's life illuminated. In matters of faith, one does not understand, then decide. Nor does one decide, then understand. Understanding is itself decision and decision is itself the form of understanding.

One ought to be wary of the distinction between historians and theologians when it is based on the historian's willingness to let the theologian take risks of judgment which he himself is unwilling to take. After discussing the history of charismatic reality in the apostolic church, Ernst Käsemann raises a question about the apostle Paul's position which bears seriously on the Christian doctrine of the church. He concludes that "the historian as such cannot answer that question." Presumably his reason is that the answer is not directly given in the data.[22] In an instance of disagreement between factions in the early church, he concludes that the historian can only weigh the reasons of both parties. "The question as to who in his historical reason (*historischen Recht*) has the actual reason (*sachliche Recht*) on his side, the theologian must answer with a personal decision."[23]

Does this mean that the task of the historian is to adduce clear evidence, and the task of the theologian is to decide in instances where the evidence is not clear? On what basis, then, would the theologian decide? Conceivably there are four possibilities:

(1) He may make a moral or metaphysical judgment which presupposes the intuition of truth not present within the historical frame of reference.

(2) He may perform an act of faith which leaps into an inevitable future dark from deficient historical illumination.

(3) He may assert a confessional judgment by which the indecisive historical data are resolved on the basis of convictions officially authoritative in the church.

(4) He may stay with the data available, continually subjecting and resubjecting them to the interpretive process, refusing to make his judgments on any other basis.

If he does the first, he has broken with theology as history. If he does the second, he is manifesting historical courage but on an a-historical basis. If he does the third, he is illustrating what most people believe theologians do. That is not entirely bad, because official church positions are crystallizations of historical meaning. They are only a-historical when they are closed to historical correction, when they have forgotten their historical origins, or when they make impersonal substitutes for acts of personal courage.

Actually, however, one who does theology within the rationality of history should be content only with the fourth possibility. Yet

[22] *Exegetische Versuche und Besinnungen*, Vol. I, p. 134.
[23] *Ibid.*, p. 187.

historians also proceed on the basis of that kind of calculated risk. When they do, it should be difficult to distinguish between the kind of judgment they make and the kind of judgment a theologian makes who does theology as history.

B. THE CATEGORIES OF HISTORICAL RATIONALITY

Beneath the form of historical understanding there is a great variety of categories at work. Categories are functions of reality which account for the possibility of its communicating itself, of its being apprehended. It is most instructive for an understanding of how one thinks historically to discern the unique historical connotations of the categories which will be adduced here. Even more instructive is the way these categories change their connotations as their context of operation is moved from one structure of reality to another and from one dimension of the structure of historical reality to another. I will single out only the most obvious. In this chapter I will illustrate the shift in the connotation of the categories as it occurs between the structures of nature and history. In the subsequent chapter I will extend the analysis to the shift between the dimensions of history from history in general through existential history to eschatological history.

Unlike the categories of Kant, historical categories are not exclusively *in the subject, in the knower.* In history the structure of understanding includes the priority of the *object,* not simply as a material given but as an intelligibility outside the knower himself, which affects the moment of understanding as actively as subjective participation does. However, it is not easy to stipulate the extent to which a category functions in the object in contrast to the extent to which it functions in the subject, because when it functions in the object, it does so as a category which once functioned in the subject. That is, when subjects contact objects, they seek out the traces of subjectivity which have become objective there. The authentication and validation of objectivity in history is thus inachievable apart from subjectivity.[24]

Time as Presence. The essential ingredient of the category of time in historical understanding is not the past. The past is reality insofar as one cannot relate to it inwardly. The past, as Sartre has said, can "haunt" the present but cannot *be* present. "The past is what I am without being able to live it."[25] If time seems to an historian a reality which, like a river, flows from the past to the future, it is only because he is standing on the bank. To the observer, history is always past. But acts of spectatorship which turn history into a spectacle convert potential historical reality into actual natural reality. Nature always exists as the past. By that I do not refer to the inevitable time lag in laboratory mechanisms for recording nature. I mean to indicate the deliberately experimental method which holds reality off at an objective distance and thus creates a gap between the time in which we live and the observed time, which is the past. History, however, always exists as the present, for meaning is temporally immediate and is not vitiated by time. In nature, not only is time computed mathematically, but the measurable moments of time are evaluated indifferently. That is, time is quantified in nature and its value is numerical. In history, time is weighed by its pertinence to ongoing life, hence moments or epochs which have the same mathematical value may have radically different "moral" value. In history, time, far from being quantified, is qualified by the human values inhering in the events it enumerates.

The genius of history as meaning is not that the past supplies a

[24] One who knows Kant and Husserl will recognize in this formulation Husserl's advance over Kant, inspired by Husserl's more active historical consciousness. J. Quentin Lauer mistakes this hermeneutical circle for a tautology. See his *The Triumph of Subjectivity*, Fordham University Press, 1958, p. 85, note 3, and p. 103, note 12. He does not fully profit from his own observations regarding Husserl's use of history (esp. pp. 56f. and 139f.), although he justly calls attention to the poverty and belatedness of historical insight in Husserl's works (p. 104). The title of Lauer's book both perpetuates the phrase and illustrates the misunderstanding of Emile

traditional foundation for the present or that the past is drawn toward the present by a process of selection and re-enactment, installing the past as a dimension of the present. History as meaning converts the spectatorial aspect of chronological time into something entirely different. The function of history as meaning is to provide human life with a structure of presence. The present as "presence" is not a mathematical point between future and past. It is rather an enduring atmosphere of significance called into existence by the presence of another reality the significance of which is enduring.

The young man in Henry James' *The Sense of the Past* learned this lesson the hard way. A citizen of the early twentieth century, he arranged to change places with an early nineteenth-century man. In the process he experienced a sense of alienation bordering on terror. Luigi Pirandello's play *Henri IV* makes the same point more brutally. A man injured in his youth has lived thereafter in the illusion that he is an eleventh-century emperor. To spare him psychological tension, his parents set him up in a castle and surrounded him with an environment exclusively reminiscent of that century. Long after his normal consciousness had returned, he continued to nurse the ruse that he was really living in the past: "In history where all is decided! Where all is fixed! . . . The joy of history!" As the play ends, there is no doubt that he knows what century he is really in; but he is nonetheless insane.

Hegel understood the alienation of the past better than Schleiermacher. For Schleiermacher, historical interpretation was a process of knowing the past better than the past knew itself. For Hegel,

---

Bréhier's *Transformation de la philosophie française*, Paris, 1950, Chapter VII, "Triomphe de la Subjectivité." There are strong traditional prejudices in Lauer's book. Nevertheless, it is an informed and lucid exposition of the main ideas of Husserl's phenomenology. Its equivalents in other languages are Maurice Merleau-Ponty, *Les Sciences de l'homme et la phenomenologie*, Paris, 1961; and Wilhelm Szilasi, *Einführung in die Phänomenologie Edmund Husserls*, Tübingen, 1959.

[25] *Being and Nothingness*, New York, 1956, p. 119.

history was present not so much in its root as in its fruit. Goethe can be cited in support of Hegel's method. In describing the historical work of his teacher, Herder, Goethe observed that Herder had not sifted gold from dirt. He had nursed the dirt of life into the form of living plants. The botanical metaphor even suggested that history may be separable from the past like fruit from the vine. Interpretations of the past, therefore, such as characterize historical acts, are not devised to guarantee the immortality of the past. They are designed to overcome the drift toward mortality in the present. History is not the nature miracle of resurrecting the past but the soteriological miracle of redeeming the present.

Memory as Self-Recollection. Memory is a sufficiently essential ingredient in the category of time to deserve independent consideration. In history where time is presence, the function of memory is *self*-recollection. As has already been established, self-recollection is not a process of inversion or introspection which turns the heart in upon itself. Self-recollection is achieved by encounter with the self-world, the human world of the past, but encounter of a sort that allows the human world there to evoke the present as meaningful. In nature the function of the memory is precisely that of self-forgetfulness, eliminating the characteristic human factor from the description of the world. In history we must, as the Epistle to the Hebrews says, "remember the prisoners as though in prison with them" (13:3). Historians who work as if within the structure of nature are characterized by Sartre in his first novel, *Nausea.* Roquentin, his hero, is in the process of writing an historical work about one Rollebon. He says of his subject, "He had need of me in order to be, and I had need of him in order not to sense my being. . . . I existed no longer in myself but in him. It is for him that I ate, for him that I breathed, each of my movements had its meaning in relation to him. . . . I was only a means of making him live, and he was my *raison d'être.* He had delivered me from myself." The sign of history, on the other hand, is not the experience of losing one's life, but of finding it. Dilthey is a surer guide than Roquentin, then, for he has claimed that "the primary condition for the possibility of the science of history is that I am myself an historical being, that the one who investigates history is the same one who makes history."[26]

Therefore, it is no longer true to say, as Francis Bacon once did, that history is based on memory while philosophy is based on reason: there is an historical reason. Nor is it true to imply that history deals with what *was* true though past and reason with what *is* true presently. The historical reason, being structured by memory, bears the responsibility for a form of self-recollection which gives history a present. That is why, despite something's happening in the past, the memory loses interest in it and cannot keep it permanently resuscitated unless it was an event that can continue to bring history into being. In the absence of that kind of resourcefulness, events "shrink to nothing as soon as they have become the past, precisely because of their uneventfulness." (Arthur Koestler)

Language as Presentation. Rationality is so inseparable from language that Hamann once said, "All chatter about reason is pure wind: language is its organ and criterion."[27] "Even if I were as eloquent as Demosthenes, I should not have to do more than thrice repeat a single phrase: Reason is language, *logos*."[28] "For me the question is not so much What is reason? as What is language?"[29]

In the structure of history the essential ingredient in the category of language is hermeneutics. "Hermeneutics" traditionally meant the science of interpretation, or how to exegete a text. While this meaning is not excluded in my use of the term, I intend the fuller implication which Heidegger's bizarre etymology brings to light. Hermeneutics, he says, is a word which derives from "Hermes," messenger of the Gods. Thus hermeneutics is not

[26] *Gesammelte Schriften*, Vol. VII, p. 278.
[27] Letter to Herder, December 8, 1783.
[28] Letter to Herder, August 6, 1784.
[29] Letter to Jacobi, Nov. 14, 1784. R. Gregor Smith, *J. G. Hamann:* A Study in Christian Existentialism, Harper, 1960, pp. 245, 246.

simply exegesis but the bringing of the message, language as presentation, that is, as making present.[30] Historical language is history interpreting itself. As such, it is not simply communication of the sort translation effects. In translation in its most restricted sense the meaning of one language is reduplicated in another. Translation is understanding *of* speech. Interpretation is understanding *in* speech. The language of history is communication not as translation but as communion. In its phrases the possibility of a presence is created. Language as interpretation is the extended moment in which one's meaning as a man is brought to expression through engagement with the structure of history. The language of interpretation is the medium in which events are able to occur with historical significance. Interpretation, then, is the process in which events live in the historian, justifying his existence, and through him in his community, justifying the existence of society.

The language of nature, like the language of translation, aims at representational exactitude. Scientific language, being the language of nature, mirrors the very structure of natural reality, so that this language can be reduced to mathematical symbols without jeopardy to the quality of the reality. Physical sciences at least are able to construct models which are the schematic representations of the mechanisms which appear in the structure of nature. The models are symbols which mirror the reality. It is wrong, however, to employ the analogy of the mirror in characterizing historical language, as medieval historians, for instance, did, following the theory of Thomas Aquinas that a word is a mirror (*speculum*) of things. Hegel used the term "representational" to describe the language of "belief without insight."[31] A faith which

[30] *Unterwegs zur Sprache*, Pfullingen, second unchanged edition, 1960, pp. 121f. After preaching at Lystra, Paul was called Hermes by the citizens "because he was the chief speaker" (Acts 14:12).

[31] *Phenomenology of Mind*, Chapter VI, pp. 549-558. Reginald O. Kapp regards what he calls "representational understanding" as irreconcilable with the "physical" structure of reality, but he does not use the word as I am using it here. For him "representation" is an act of imagination by which

is historical and therefore also meaningful cannot exist at the level of representational language. For history, like fine arts, is not a representational language but a presentational language. It contains the reality it describes.

The most ancient forms of Christian art, the forms closest to our Lord in time, are non-representational in character, like today's abstract art. The most enduring form of medieval art, cathedral windows, even though depicting Biblical scenes, are by intention non-representational, for they were not meant to be looked at, as tourists do with the aid of binoculars. They are flashes of light and color in the walls of the cathedral, resembling fireworks bursting in a night sky. They luminously pattern the Christian's life with meaning by celebrating the event in which one's history is continually being created. Surely it is not simply an accident of amateur photography when one's colored slides of the rose window at Rheims are almost indistinguishable from one's slides of the fireworks celebrating the fall of the Bastille on July 14th.

Galileo was right, then, to observe that nature is written in mathematical language. It does not alter the meaning of natural language that these symbols are structured by man's own subjective activity, as Leibnitz, Kant, and Cassirer have contended. Ernst Cassirer's sustained attack upon a merely "copy" theory of language in natural science does not substantially affect the thesis that, in the structure of nature, language represents reality as it is in its objectivity, as it is where the question of meaning for man is not raised. Not that the language of science is devoid of subjective structures. One can cite the view of Herder, as Cassirer does, to the effect that language is "the reflection not of an objective environment, but of man's own life and action," or of von Humboldt that "the word is not a copy of an object as such, but re-

---

objective reality is re-imaged, and in the process somewhat subjectivized. When I say "representation" I mean just the opposite, namely, the disciplined effort to reproduce nature linguistically by consciously eliminating subjectivity. Cf. *Towards a Unified Cosmology*, London, 1960, pp. 175ff.

flects the soul's image of the object."[32] But if "man's own life and action" and "images of the soul" do not originate or participate in concern for significance in life, they belong as much to the structure of nature as do naked objects.

This distinction is not meant to be pejorative. It is the vocation of natural science to isolate nature from history. To that end natural language strives toward freedom from historical language, which is language structured not simply by the subject but by the subject concerned about the meaning of existence. It is true that a merely imitative intention requires and includes subjective effort which makes of language not a simple mirroring of reality but an active reconstruction of it. All that can be said of what occurs in the structure of nature. The *mimesis* of history, however, is not a reconstruction of reality but a dramatic personal participation in reality. Mathematical formulae require reconstruction by anyone who would understand them. History, however, requires participation as a basis for understanding. The language of the structure of nature requires reconstruction of the sort an actor gives his part in a drama. Drama is a mimetic art, an imitative art. That does not mean the dramatist need not "throw himself into" the part, reconstructing it intelligibly, adding something of his own in order to reduplicate a Hamlet or a Job. History, however, is not a histrionic but a kerygmatic art. The historian does not throw himself mimetically into the parts which have been played. He stands back from them in order to estimate their effect, then transcribes that effect. Dramatists and scientists who read the script of the storming the Bastille will raise their voices with the mob. Historians and preachers, hearing the mob, will repeat their cries in a voice subdued by reflection on the enormity of the event. One can tell, for instance, whether a Christian lives in nature or in history by the way he reads the scriptures aloud. If he screams with the mob, "Crucify him!", the chances are fairly certain that he is one who

[32] Ernst Cassirer, *The Philosophy of Symbolic Forms*, Yale University Press, Vol. I, 1953 (translated from the German edition of 1923 by Ralph Manheim), pp. 285 and 284, respectively.

naturalizes his faith, casting it in the language of representation. If he repeats those cries in a voice dazed and muffled by the pathetic constellation of events which led to the crucifixion, the chances are that he is conceiving his faith historically.[33]

The language of history, then, ought not be classed with just any kind of written record. Historical documents are not comparable to seismographic charts or mathematical models through which the explosive power of history is registered at second hand. Historical documents are themselves history; they carry in themselves the explosive power of the events they delineate. The Peloponnesian wars are contemporary wars to the extent that Thucydides lived their tragedy and expressed that life in documents through which we now relive them. When one reads the private diaries of the citizens and rulers involved in the American Revolution either he relives the Revolution or he may safely judge that the documents are not history and may relegate them to the secondary bibliography. Historical writings, therefore, are not symbolic in the paradoxical sense of being the presence of something absent. They are the presence. Nor are they merely witness in the sense that a witness is believed to be the indispensable reporter of an event, yet nothing in himself. Historical witnesses are present to history in such a way that history exists in them. Without their witness, there is no history. History, like music and poetry, *is* in its expression. At this very moment all history exists either in the

[33] Cf. Martin Heidegger, *Unterwegs zur Sprache*, p. 254: "Speaking is at the same time hearing. . . . It is a hearing of the speaking that we speak. . . . We not only speak the language; we speak *out* of it." Kierkegaard and Bonhoeffer had already expressed this view of language in relation to how to preach and how to read the Bible aloud. See Bonhoeffer's *Life Together* and *The Witness of Kierkegaard*, edited by Carl Michalson, Association Press, 1960, pp. 107-111. Cf. also K. E. Lögstrup, *Kierkegaards und Heideggers Existenzanalyse und ihr Verhältnis zur Verkündigung*, Berlin, 1950. For the same type of problem in its relation to the later works of Heidegger, see Heinrich Ott, *Denken und Sein*, Der Weg Martin Heideggers und der Weg der Theologie, Zurich, 1959. Cf. Ott's brochure, *Verkündigung und Existenz*, 1956.

living memory of those who know it or in some documentary form—a scroll, a vase, a fossil or a ruin. If through some evil genie all such witness were suddenly to be dissolved, history would at that instant drop into oblivion. Whatever one may believe about nature's capacity to exist without anyone to notice it, history is nothing apart from the language through which it survives.

The presentational character of historical language marks the difference between historical knowledge and psychological knowledge by taking history out of the area of introspection. It marks the difference between historical knowledge and physical knowledge by taking history out of the area of retrospection, assuming the time of nature to be the past. For the same reasons a faith which is historically discerned will be neither introspective, a kind of *fides qua creditur*, nor retrospective, a *fides quae creditur*. History is rather an event so structured that within it the language by which the past lives in the present evokes one's presence.

The works of the German theologians, Ernst Fuchs and Gerhard Ebeling, are enormously instructive at this point. For Ebeling, speech is not an object one analyzes but an event through which one understands. The theological significance of this formulation of "speech-event" is indeed far-reaching. Jesus can be said to be a "speech-event" who identifies himself with his words. The word of God is not a language in detachment from God but the very coming of God himself. For Fuchs, primitive Christianity is a speech phenomenon, and the very possibility for thinking the Christian faith is given in the New Testament, itself a new style in language.[34]

The theology of Fuchs and Ebeling is sometimes referred to as post-Bultmann. It is true that the word "demythologizing," which is the hallmark of the Bultmann theology, rarely appears in their recent writings. However, the concept of the "speech-event" is directly dependent upon what Bultmann means by "de-

[34] See Gerhard Ebeling, *Wort und Glaube*, Tübingen, 1960, especially pp. 244, 333, 369, and 457; Ernst Fuchs, *Zur Frage nach dem historischen Jesus*, Tübingen, 1960, especially pp. 261 and 263.

mythologizing." One characteristic of the mythologizing tendency as it appears in the New Testament writings is its way of expressing the word of God in the form of general truths. "Son of God"? Gnostic mythology had already expressed that truth. "Second coming of Jesus"? Apocalyptic Judaism was already anticipating a future messiah. "Dying and rising Savior"? The Hellenistic mystery religions everywhere knew about that kind of religious phenomenon. "God's word given to his people"? The religion of the Old Testament knew that reality. There the people were accustomed to going to their prophets to hear what God had said. The uniqueness of the New Testament message, however, is that Jesus is God's word to us. One does not formulate general truths about him, as christological theories tend to do and as the New Testament itself does, borrowing the myths of Gnosticism, of apocalyptic Judaism, and of the Hellenistic mysteries. One preaches him. When one does a theology instead of preaching, one does a theology concerning him whose reality is precisely that he is to be preached. The point is not to speak *about* God or Christ but so to speak of Christ that God himself can speak in that event of speaking. "Speech-event" is a method of speaking in which speech not simply describes an event which has happened. It creates an event. Even unlike the Old Testament, the "speech-event" is not a word given once upon a time to the prophets in the past, which the prophets thereafter declare to us. It is a word which when repeated creates our present. As Bultmann says it, the word and history occur together. That is the truth of the Christian faith which theologies of incarnation and redemption intend to indicate: God became speech in human history in order to create a history. A "speech-event" is an event of speech which constitutes one's very history. "Speech-event" in these regards is not a uniquely Christian phenomenon but merely a properly historical phenomenon. It would only be deplorable if Christianity were a fully historical faith, yet did not avail itself of the historical categories which make that faith historically meaningful.

The extent to which the communication of a faith is reliant

upon the development of a language is startling. Before early Christianity could spread to Europe, it had to teach Europe how to understand Latin, not because the missionaries were too sluggish to appropriate the barbarian languages, but because the barbarian languages were too poverty-stricken to admit one to the fullest comprehension of the faith. Before the Protestant reform was achieved in Germany and France, Luther and Calvin reformed the languages of their people, and by that act became as impressive in philological circles as in theological circles. Luther's friendship for humanism was linked with his hostility toward the spiritualist sects of the reform. This is an important fact for theology as history. One of the major reasons for Luther's alliance with secular scholarship against the forces of fanaticism was the humanist's appreciation of language. The spiritualist believed that the spirit of God, while expressed in human language, is independent of language. Luther stood against this cleavage by insisting that while the spirit is not identical with language, it is inseparable from it. In the degree in which humanism insisted on disciplined language study, it was considered by Luther an ally of God in the Reformation. Sound language study is a basis for sound doctrine. Augustine in his treatise on education, *De doctrina Christiana*, had extolled a knowledge of Greek, Hebrew, and Latin, but, as Luther pointed out, he made serious mistakes in his exegesis of the Psalms for want of an adequate knowledge of Hebrew. Luther believed that his time had a better understanding of the Gospel than did the fathers of the church, chiefly because of advances that had been made in language study. At least for that reason he refused to concede to the early fathers a normative role in Christian belief.[35]

If one appreciates that sacred literature like history is the form in which the acts of the gods have their being, and not mere reports of moments which have occurred at another time, one can appreciate the concern of Christianity to keep the Bible at the center of Christian reflection. The critical error of religious move-

[35] See Peter Meinhold, *Luthers Sprachphilosophie*, Berlin, 1958, esp. Chapters III and IV.

ments, however, is to regard its literature as representational, in which case its language, like scientific language, tends to become a substitute for its objects of devotion. The importance of historical language as presentational is not that it represent reality but that it re-present that reality, bringing it into communion with those to whom it is presented, elucidating the meaning of their existence. Biblical language is historically accurate, therefore, not when it accurately reflects the situation of the past, but when it does for the present what it did for the past.

Society as Community. A man's consciousness of history dawns upon him in the instant in which he becomes aware of membership in a group. The bearer of history is society. That fact intimately relates society to the category of language, for society's role in bearing history is essentially linguistic. The sixteenth-century French historian, Jean Bodin, called attention to this when he named Moses as the only Biblical historian to classify with the authors of universal history. He cited Moses' charge to his followers. "You will tell all these things to your sons," he said, because according to Bodin, "Moses anticipated the destruction of his books." Society is what Raymond Aron calls "the objective mind" of history, or what might more vitalistically be called the living tradition. Its role is to emerge from the past in such a way as to make the future possible.

Society is an important concept in the structure of nature as well. All scientific discovery profits by the history of man's experience with nature and by dialogue in the scientific community. However, nature can be intuited directly, like mathematical ideas. Mediation by society is helpful but not necessary to it. That is because nature is made of particulars which are classifiable in species and genera. History is made of individuals who are related in society. One can arrive at the particulars of nature by intuiting the species and genus. The social character of nature is never more than classification. One can arrive at the individuals of history, however, only by entering into dialogue in community. That distinctive character of history is most strikingly noticed in the reaction which its data elicit. The data of the structure of nature establish liaisons as of a subject with an object. Historical reality involves quite a different reaction. Its realities are more like selves than like objects. They address us, evoking our response.

Historical language is primarily a social concept, therefore. It is not the representation of an object, signifying something which it is not, as in science. Nor is it the expression of a subject which denies extant objects in order to prepare the way for new realities, as in art.

History as a method of relating to reality is located somewhere between science and art. History is neither as objective as science, which defines itself by its objectivity, nor as subjective as art, which defines itself by its subjectivity. History is man's subjective penetration into objects which exist by virtue of their subjectivity, their meaning for man. Thus history enjoys the status of friend of man, while both science and art appear sooner or later as enemies of man, although for quite different reasons. The warning to the rationality of faith, which is implicit in this position of history should be taken seriously. Theological alliances with or analogies to either science or art tend to weaken the full historicity of theology and thus, in some sense, the full significance of the Christian faith.

Because of its exceptional objectivity natural expression never achieves the status of history. Because of its exceptional subjectivity, artistic language never achieves the status of history, not even when it is depicting historical scenes. Gericault's "Raft of the Medusa," Goya's "The Third of May," David's "Coronation of Napoleon" and Delacroix's classical themes are not interested in the event which supplies the content of their pictures.

Artists who seem to deal in history are not historians, but, as Croce has called them, "palimpsests." Their interpretations are "new expressions imposed upon the ancient, artistic fancies instead of historical reproductions."[36] Charles Ives' "Concord

[36] *Aesthetic*, Noonday Press, p. 127.

Sonata" is comprised of allusions to United States history. Darius Milhaud wrote an opera with Paul Claudel's libretto on Christopher Columbus. Nevertheless, despite these very direct suggestions of historiography in music, we have to do in these works with art and not with history. How different the criterion of art is from the criterion of history can be seen in the following candid judgment: "The general criterion for judging the authenticity of a work of art consists in the fact that it coincides exactly with the intention of the author."[37] The truth of the phenomenological axiom that intention always corresponds to some object is not denied by this canon of aesthetic subjectivity. Abstractionists point to their canvases as the object of their intention. In a sense, historians point to their writings as the object of their intention, for history exists in historical writing. But in history historical objects have also pre-existed the historian's subjectivity. Art, on the other hand, even when it seems to rely on pre-existing objects, actually inheres in the *de novo* character of the aesthetic object. Arnold Schoenberg summarizes the subjectivity, novelty, and creativity of art in his characterization of a musical chord. "A new chord is a symbol involuntarily invented and reveals the new man who is expressed by it."[38]

Science copies. Art creates. History interprets. Historical language as interpretation rejects the gap between the subject and the object in order to relate them. Yet it does so without ever relinquishing either its fidelity to the object or its creative subjective responsibility to negate the object. The dialectical relation between subject and object in history is not an ordinary subject-object relation such as occurs in the monologue with nature. It is genuine dialogue, constituted by the fact that history is a record of a personal sort. The distinctive thing about history is neither

[37] Alois Haba, *Von Neuer Musik,* Cologne, 1924, cited by H. H. Stuckenschmidt, *Musique Nouvelle,* Paris, 1956, p. 288. Translated from the German by Jean-Claude Salel.

[38] *Ibid.,* p. 306. Cf. Henry Miller, *The Wisdom of the Heart,* New Directions Paperbook, 1960, p. 3, "The artist . . . is always a-historical."

loyalty to objective facts nor expression of subjective imagination but response to the subjectivity in the objects, which is their social, human character.

In distinguishing art from history I am consciously augmenting the aesthetic of Susanne Langer with the Sartrean understanding of the essentially nihilating character of conscious acts. "All art is the creation of perceptible forms expressive of human feeling."[39] But the hidden intentionality in the artistic expression of human feeling can be called creative because it is directed not toward objects which exist but toward objects which do not exist. The implication of creation, therefore, is annihilation, in the sense in which one annihilates the other patrons of a restaurant while looking only for Pierre, and even annihilates Pierre while looking only for one's image of Pierre. History is less violent than art because it is not allowed this exclusively subjective creation by nihilation. In this understanding, abstract art can be considered as the most characteristic realization of art, for it is the most complete realization of creative subjectivity accomplished by virtue of the most complete denial of any prior objectivity.

What Jean-Paul Sartre has said of the voluptuousness of Baudelaire can be said of art. "Being against the established order, and exercizing a freedom which is condemned in order to be born, it seems analogous to creation."[40] Sartre demonstrates his awareness of the drift of art away from history, however, when he calls attention to Baudelaire's voyeurism. As Baudelaire himself said,

[39] Susanne K. Langer, *Problems of Art*, Scribners, 1957, p. 80. Cf. R. G. Collingwood, *Speculum Mentis*, Oxford, 1924, p. 91: "Art thinks of itself as a pure act of imagination, cut off and disconnected from anything outside itself." The statement is made in paragraph 6 entitled "Art as a form of error." See also Jean Genêt's even more provocative statement: "No doubt it is one of the functions of art to replace faith by the effective ingredient of beauty. At least this beauty must have the power of a poem, that is to say of a crime," as "in the sacrifice of the Mass. The starting point disappears under the profusion of ornaments and symbols." Cited by Martin Esslin, *The Theatre of the Absurd*, Anchor Book, 1961, p. 149.

[40] *Baudelaire*, Paris, 1947, p. 85.

"To have sexual intercourse is to aspire to penetrate another, and the artist never leaves himself." The artist is, as Sartre says of Baudelaire, a voyeur and fetichist who possesses reality from a distance.[41] Not as the scientist, who lets reality be an object, but as one who never fondles objects which he has not created. The historian, between the scientist and the artist, knows reality, as Biblical history says we can—namely, as Adam knew Eve. Whenever Baudelaire made love, he wore gloves. The hands of the scientist are gloved to keep the subject from contaminating the object; the hands of the artist are gloved to keep the object from overpowering the subject. Only the hands of the historian are bared so that the subject may establish contact with the object.

One may wonder if the emphasis on the presence of history in language does not rather deny such intimate participation to history and thus to religious experience. Does a lover know his beloved only in the mediation of language? Was not Schleiermacher, then, justified to limit his courtship to the medium of correspondence? The position looks exceedingly ungratifying when placed on that plane. Surely the meeting of I and thou in an act of love enjoys an intimacy in which even the *spoken* word seems obtrusive. What must it be to meet only at the level of the *written* word, if not like lovers furtively exchanging notes but never touching?

The price the Christian faith pays for being historical is not to be immediate. There is no immediate relation of a Christian sort between Christians: Christians are mediated into community by the ministry of the word. There is no immediate relation between Christians and their Lord: that relation is mediated by the witness of the community, the church. There is no immediate relation between Christians and God: that relation is mediated by Jesus of Nazareth, the word of God. However, the apparent dis-

[41] *Ibid.*, p. 88. Martin Heidegger's understanding of art is a-historical in a different sense from the line I have taken here. For my evaluation of his understanding of the relation of art and history see my essay, "Theology as Ontology and as History," in the volume edited by James Robinson and John Cobb, *The Later Heidegger and Theology*, Harper, 1963.

advantage of historical mediacy turns to advantage when it is known that there are no Christian relationships which are not meaningful in the sense in which history is meaningful. History is not simply the having of experiences but the having of meaningful experiences, experiences which are acts interpreting themselves in word. In faith, then, the blind and voiceless acts of love, the spiritual blackouts and eroticism which many Christians undergo are not normative, for faith being historical enjoys the rational love of history, which is intimacy with reality insofar as it is meaningfully mediated. In history, a faith relation will never be erotic, but it will nevertheless always be a speaking relation.

Decision as Risk. The essential ingredient of the category of decision in history is risk. The time of presence which exists in the language of interpretation actualizes itself in history through the risk of decision. In nature there are decisions but there are no risks. Security is a legitimate expectation of nature, even though contacts with nature do not always inspire it, revealing chaos and calamity as well as orderliness. In the past, when the chaos of nature has terrified the human spirit, man has been tempted to historicize nature, as is evidenced in the ease with which he has moved back and forth between control over nature and deification or demonization of nature. Mythology arises as humanity's historical compromise with the menacing disorderliness of nature. The characteristic stance in the structure of nature, however, remains the sense of orderliness, of which the psychological derivative is security and the vocational derivative technology. Nature is given to be dominated. What one dominates becomes his technological object. When one dominates, he feels secure.

The characteristics which are intrinsic to the structure of nature are alien to the structure of history, for a man's relation to nature does not involve the man himself as his relation to history does. The truth of nature, therefore, is an attribute of the correspondence of a language with a reality outside man himself. In history, on the other hand, truth is an attribute of the correspondence of a language with man's own reality as well. That is, history exists in a mode of interpretation called language. The interpretation is history insofar as it is capable of bringing the meaning of man's existence to expression, or, what is the same, of conferring on man a presence.

The question, "Is it true or false?" is not the only test of validity to which to subject historical experience. One of the clearest analyses of this problem is provided in the writings of Wilhelm Dilthey. According to Dilthey there are three modes in which life may express itself, and there is a different test of validity for each mode. These three classes of expression are sentences, acts, and experiential expressions. Sentences, which are concepts or intellectual judgments, have no necessary relation to experience. They embody the pure content of thought and best lend themselves to the tests of formal logic, the test of coherence. The test of validity in this class is the question, "Is it true or false?"—that is, "Do the sentences agree?" A second class of experience is actions, such as the making or the use of a tool. Here one does not ask, is the act true or false? One asks, is it suitable or unsuitable? Validity in acts is defined by suitability to projected ends. The third class is called experiential expressions. This sphere is the most appropriate to human understanding. It is the sphere of history. One may ask the question of true and false or the question of suitability, but there is still a deeper and more intrinsic question. In history one does not have an adequate test of validity if he stops short of the question of authenticity and inauthenticity. I take the distinction to mean that in history, validity is determined by the ability of statements, which necessarily articulate human experience, to bring human experience to expression in some fundamentally meaningful form.[42]

[42] See the discussion in Otto Friedrich Bollnow, *Dilthey:* Eine Einführung in seine Philosophie, second edition, Stuttgart, 1955 (first edition, 1936), pp. 181-191. The distinction between authenticity and inauthenticity has been expressed by Martin Heidegger in the terms *Eigentlichkeit* and *Uneigentlichkeit*. Dilthey had already expressed the distinction in the terms *Wahrhaftigkeit* and *Unwahrhaftigkeit* (p. 186).

Reason in the structure of nature may oblige us to accept the conclusions of a syllogism whose premises have been admitted. Reason in the structure of history obliges us to exist, to be ourselves, *as* the conclusions of premises which are rationally incomplete without us. Syllogistically, conclusions have a kind of pre-existence in their premises. Historically, premises are invocations to conclusions which are indeterminable in advance. Historical thinking is less in the form of syllogistic reasoning and more in the form which *Haiku* poetry took in its early development. The Japanese poet posed lines which, left unfinished, placed upon the auditor the responsibility for completion. History like art at its best always has this invocational quality. In history as in the appreciation of a work of art one is dealing with unclosed events where the encounter and resolution become parts of the event.[43]

The presence of meaning is necessarily fulfilled, therefore, in acts of decision, acts by which truths which are potentially exterior, thus subject to leaping into the order of nature, become interiorized, thus guaranteeing their status as history. Not that one simply decides this or that in history is true, as if there were some criterion outside history by which to determine its truth. Rather, in decision one consents that this moment of interpretation is the moment of lucidity in which he is brought to existence. That he so decides without the objective assurances of nature is his risk. Refusal to take such risks would constitute a betrayal of history. The seriousness of the betrayal is in the fact that history, unlike nature, does not hurtle forward by inertia. History survives through the mediation of language which does not come into existence without the human decision. In nature one is responsible for reducing risk to its lowest frequency. In history, risk is of the essence. One assumes it joyfully, therefore, but with courage.

Historical responsibility carries a terrifying implication which is not present in art. In art one may return day after day to the same images and meditate endlessly in the quiet of the museum,

[43] Cf. Hans-Georg Gadamer, *Wahrheit und Methode*, Grundzüge einer philosophischen Hermeneutik, Tübingen, 1960, p. 94.

protracting his decision. In history, the image does not wait. One must decide in an instant, as one decides in motoring past roadside signs. Albert Camus tells a savage tale which must be meant to signify this burden of decision in history. It is called "Cross Purposes" (*Le Malentendu*). A young husband returns home from a long absence, unannounced and disguised in order to enjoy the slow emergence of surprise in his wife and her mother. Meanwhile the wife and mother, left at home to run the family hotel, have planned to kill and rob their next guest to gain the means of travel to see the young husband. While their guest searches for the right word with which to greet his hostesses, they kill him. As Camus writes, "While searching for his words, he was killed." In history, filibuster can be fatal.

Power as Freedom. History is the effect of momentous forces. To conclude the discussion of its categories on so slender an influence as risk of decision leaves one with the uneasy feeling that such a mouse could never have mothered all the mountains on our historical horizons. Surely the currents of history are only imperceptibly deflected by human decisions. Its energies must be more recognizable in the bulky and emphatic realities of fate, destiny and providence, than they are in the relatively lilliputian realities of self-realization, vocabulary and decision. Is not the validity of the definition of history as meaning subject to the question of its capacity to account for the "forces" of history?

One is inclined to become diverted by this line of questioning until he senses in it a throwback to the pugilistic dialogue between the young sons of the village blacksmith and the village poet. Whose father is the stronger? The meaning of the word "power" is split down the middle by the structures of nature and history. It is not a question of which structure is more powerful because power is defined by the structure and not vice versa. The power of the glacial age which heaped up the Alps in Europe and subsequently created the possibility of Swiss neutrality has no history in it. The power of the Goths demolishing Rome has less history in it than the power of the Romans civilizing Europe. Whatever powers, chemical and physical, have formed the universe, they are not historical powers. They still leave man seeking an understanding, a motive other than nature by which to accept what this ambiguous power has thrown up.

Power in nature is physically computable force. Power in history is the freedom to use and shape these forces toward meaningful ends. Natural power can thwart historical power, as when avalanches bury cities or *Realpolitik* based on blood exterminates a people. But historical power can conquer natural power. When a people extends its boundaries by military force, the world witnesses natural power with historical consequences. When a people extends its boundaries by dredging the sea from its shores and extending its fields, the world witnesses historical power with natural consequences. One cannot say the poet has *more* power than the blacksmith because in doing so he equivocates with the word "power," leaping over the line between nature and history. But one can say that the power of the blacksmith is at the disposal of the poet in a way in which the contrary is not true. None of the power of history is available to nature, yet all of the power of nature is available to history. One ought never say that history belongs to the natural process, but it is permissible to say, as Karl Marx did, that "nature and its transformations belong to the historical process."[44] The "power" which the Christian laity unleashed in the crusades was historical power because formed in the beneficence of the reforms of Gregory VII and of Cluny monasticism. The "power" which Cromwell unleashed was historical power because formed in the democratic spirit of puritanism which prevailed in the masses of the underprivileged.[45] History as meaning, which is a constant appeal to the relatively poetic force of intelligent, self-conscious freedom, is weak only in the sense that a lever is weak when, applied to a fulcrum, it moves a burden utterly disproportionate to the force applied. "The dynamo

[44] Robert Tucker's lucid formulation of Karl Marx's comprehensive historicism, *Philosophy and Myth in Karl Marx*, Cambridge University Press, 1961, p. 23.

[45] Droysen, *Historik*, p. 200.

and the virgin" are both "forces" in history. But as Henry Adams said, "all the steam in the world could not, like the Virgin, build Chartres." Therefore it is not implausible to the author of the Epistle to the Hebrews, reviewing the history which culminated in the Christian movement, that "by faith the walls of Jericho fell down" (Hebrews 11:30). Within these structures of understanding it is meaningful to say that "with God, all things are possible" (Matthew 19:26).

My purpose in this discussion has not been to tell the historian how to handle his data. Rather, I have attempted to learn from historical methodology how theologians may more adequately handle theirs, considering that their data is essentially historical. Whatever the historian may think about how these things relate to how they do their work, I am myself exhilarated by their implications for how theologians do theirs. More so, I am exhilarated by the implications for how Christians in general may understand their life of faith, some aspects of which have remained burdensome, anxiety-ridden, and thus hostile to the interests of a liberating faith.

Christian faith is of the structure of history. That means one holds his faith in a structure with very precise characteristics. A life of faith like a life of history is an interworld between two poles, a subject and an object. The subjective pole is a sentiment for meaning which haunts the human life and gives it a projection outward for some reality which can fulfill its expectations. "Faith" in New Testament understanding exists neither as capitulation to objective realities nor as a subjective passion. Faith is always "faith in" or "belief on." Faith exists only with the aid of a prepositional outreach which ties it to a reality beyond the believer while tying the reality beyond the believer to the believer. This structure is very similar to what phenomenologists have called the "intentional" structure of consciousness. As they say, consciousness is never simply a state of consciousness; it is always a consciousness of a state. Historians also have known for a long time that history is a reality which emerges only in relation to the historian as interlocutor. History, like philosophy, is always completed in some corresponding movement of reality toward the human consciousness.

The sentiment of the subjective question when left unsatisfied is the source of every kind of fanaticism religiously and culturally, for it is a dearth in the human spirit. Unquenched, it inspires either rebellion or hallucination. Subjective hunger for meaning breaks rebelliously with cultural institutions which offer stones for bread, but it also invents alternatives as thirsty desert travellers invent oases. The tradition of a faith is the objective pole of the interworld of history. It resolves rebellious and hallucinatory passions without destroying their authentic origins. For there in history one can find the witness to meanings which correspond to the human quest for meaning. History for the Christian is the interworld of meaning constituted by events which embrace God's word to man and man's obedient response. God's word is history because it occurs in such a way as to supply meaning. Man's faith is history because it is the response of obedience to God which has its correlate in man's own quest for meaning. "Acts of God," like floods, are nature and therefore meaningless to man. Acts of God addressed to man, like covenants, are history. They do not strike the surface of man's life as lightning strikes a tree. They touch man's life as decipherable sounds strike ear-drums. Assimilation is possible. In history that process of assimilation is called communion. When the decipherable sounds of the tradition of faith are heard, they are heard not as an echo from the past but as a call to be present. They appear not as the surrogate of a reality remote but as the presentation of that reality. They inspire not the banal sense that all things now are solid underneath. The everlasting arms are made of history, the fleshiness of the lived world. That means they are near and they are meaningful and our souls are made to be embraced by them. But it also means we will never be comfortable in their embrace as one is comfortable in repose. One sinks in repose once and for all. One is embraced by everlasting arms in the recurrence of affirmation and consent.

Repentance, conversion and confession are as comprehensible

to faith, therefore, as the risk of interpretation is to history in general, and in the same way. They are born of the interworld of history where the sentiment for meaning is satisfied by the meaningful context which religious tradition sediments in sacred writings and institutions. Like history, however, this sedimentation has the authority not of a norm but of a frame of reference, not of lightning in its force but of lightning in its illumination. Canonicity and apostolicity as criteria of truth in the church do not connote a formal privilege. These certain apostles or these certain documents do not hold the truth as once and for all given and directly channeled now to us. Canonicity and apostolicity mean an actual responsibility. The truth of Christian history can be lost for want of a witness to interpret it. Formal privileges cannot be lost; that is their seductive advantage. Actual responsibilities can wither away from atrophy or abuse. That is their deceptive weakness. Christians like historians must learn to trade seductive advantages for deceptive weaknesses. For as in history, so in faith there is no meaning apart from documents and witnesses; yet in history these instruments survive by virtue of their capacity to be historical, to present meaning, to bring existence into expression. The church as history can cease to exist, notwithstanding its formal apostolate and official book, if the actual historical responsibility of this traditional form is in default. Protestantism once held that threat against the church in its medieval form. Sectarian groups had done so against the "great church" since its beginning. The world, however, has always held this threat against the church and does so now. "What gives your view authority?" The religions of antiquity promised freedom to the people through the ministry of the state. When the state ceased granting freedom, the religions died. Christianity is the promise of meaningful existence. Its survival is rightfully in question wherever the church fails to contribute sense to the life of the people. The world will contribute to a Christian's sense of history if it refuses to be put off by formal assurances which do not illuminate.

CHAPTER 3

FAITH AS HISTORICAL MATURITY

The most real event is the one which most imposes itself upon the consciousness as an organizing center of the historical process.

PIERRE THÉVENAZ, *L'Homme et sa Raison,* Vol. II, Raison et histoire, Neuchâtel, 1956, p. 136.

The question which theology today can no longer evade . . . is the question of history. And it is put to theology in a completely new way precisely through eschatology.

FRIEDRICH GOGARTEN, *Verhängnis und Hoffnung der Neuzeit,* Stuttgart, 1953, second edition 1958, pp. 180 and 194.

THERE is a rationality of nature and a rationality of history. To apply the canons of one to the medium of the other is to initiate conflicts expressible as paradox or contradiction. The conflicts are not essentially related either to history or to nature, for neither of these media is inherently against reason. That is, neither nature nor history requires a man to surrender some aspect of his native ability to understand. Such conflicts are rather the direct result of mixing the methods of nature with the methods of history.

The Christian faith is an essentially historical reality embracing acts of faith as historical responses to God's self-manifestation in history. The faith is not inherently irrational. That is, one does not violate the integrity of his power of understanding in becoming a Christian. Faith is only made to seem irrational when methods of reflection which are inappropriate to it are employed in appropriating it, that is, when its essentially historical structure is subjected to implements of understanding which are properly the property of the structure of nature. The supposed irrationality of faith can be traced to confusion in methods of appropriation and not to the faith itself. By the canons of nature, history is irrational because its structure is filled with human ambiguities which elude exact measurement. By the canons of history, nature is irrational because it does not address itself to the paramount concern of human rationality which is concern for meaning. Hence, when faith, an historical phenomenon, is subjected to the methods of natural discernment, it seems as irrational as historical phenomena do in general. Yet when faith emerges, it does so as the redeemer of the irrationality of a life lived on the plane of nature alone.

The story of the rationality of faith cannot be ended on this cool and calculated level of truce, however, for history carries within itself certain threats of irrationality of its own. The rationality of history is the rationality of meaning. Yet the very existence of a structure of meaning implies a judgment on itself. Is the hope for meaning, which history incites, historically realizable? Does history experience any moments of fertility which can give a presence to human life? Are there meanings through which history coheres notwithstanding the sense of granulation in history? In the light of history, nature is a threatening irrationalism, for it sponsors structures of power which have *no* meaning in them. In the light of history's own promise of meaning, however, does not history emerge as a tantalizing irrationalism, quickening a thirst for meaning which it does not itself quench?

I. HISTORICITY AS THE LOGIC OF MEANINGLESSNESS

"Historicity" is the name for "the history of what the normal historian passes over" . . . "a host of seeming-trivial details" . . . "Intrinsically ugly" . . . "bits of conversation overheard in trams and in the streets," namely, how the people work, love, and die.[1] The term "historicity" labels existential history, the dimension of history in which it is revealed that history itself may be deficient in meaning and possibly even finally uninhabitable. "Historicity" is a term which has customarily been taken to signify the factuality of an event. In contemporary thought the meaning of the term has transmigrated far beyond this popular connotation. Its first major shift came with Wilhelm Dilthey who said in a letter to Count von Yorck, "The nub of historicity is that the whole of reality *is* not but lives." That is, historicity is history happening in such a way that one can actually live it. Martin Heidegger gave the term its second turn in saying that the nub of historicity is neither that the whole of reality *is* nor that it *lives* but that it dies. That is, historicity is history happening in such a way as to raise a serious question as to whether one can really live there. Heidegger found his basis for this revision in Dilthey's own description of human life as temporality. Temporality is the continual perishing of time into the death of sheer pastness. Nevertheless, Heidegger's

[1] Albert Camus, *The Plague*, Penguin Books, p. 23.

redefinition is distinctive. It means that historical thinking cannot be based on the methods of nature, which lack subjective concern; it cannot even be based on subjective concern unless that concern has been intensified by the question of whether there is ultimate meaning, defying death. Immanuel Kant had answered the question of the significance of life with the postulate of immortality. Heidegger requires his philosophy to proceed with the same question but without invoking that postulate. The consequence is the experience of historicity. How can there be a history, a fundamentally meaningful life, where threats of meaninglessness seem to have the last word?

"Historicity" refers to the tension in history in which history's capacity to supply man with a presence is most in question. By historicity, therefore, is no longer meant the factuality of historical claims. That question has been taken over by the fundamentally a-historical sciences. History is life with a presence, that is, life with meaning. Historicity is history's own exposure of the absence in history of anything to provide the grounds for a presence. The possibility of continuity in life is not something in man, as the older metaphysics tended to affirm. The ground of man's continuity is in history. If man were a nature whose structure were given and whose givenness were a permanence, subject perhaps to exposure and injury, but not to ultimate disintegration, historicity would be an illusion. But on these same terms history itself would be impossible. Man is not a given nature but an existence, a presence, a history whose capacity to survive does not relate to preestablished structures but to satisfaction of fundamental needs. Man is reducible to his needs, as Sartre says.[2] Needs, humanly defined, are historical. Man feeds on meaning, and where there is no meaning he dies far in advance of his interment. That is why Hegel could say of the human consciousness, it is "a hole in being."[3] Man's quest for meaning punctures the terrain of history

[2] *Critique de la raison dialectique*, Vol. I, Paris, 1960, pp. 202-208.

[3] Cited by Maurice Merleau-Ponty, *La Structure du Comportement*, Paris, third edition, 1953, p. 136.

like fabricated basins in drought-stricken fields, waiting for rain. There is a scarcity at the base of history. The scarcity includes the literal hunger, poverty, and corrosive vices which decimate the body, and the death which terminates it. The scarcity includes aggressive elements of exploitation which aggravate the poverty and wars[4] which accelerate death's otherwise well-regulated timetable. Man is the instrument and man the victim in history. Man is the breach of meaninglessness, the source of history's aggressive irrationality. Man is the weaver of the web of cross-purposes upon which he is himself entrapped. The story of his life includes the annals of the dead in wars, case histories of the dying in psychiatric wards, diaries of composers who never heard their works performed. One will know the meaning of historicity if one knows why Voltaire was nauseated by history: it is a document about man which resembles a police report, yet, far from manifesting penitence, congratulates itself. On the day of the liberation of the Bastille the King of France scratched only one word in his diary: "Nothing." One will know the difference between history and historicity if one recognizes in that word, "nothing," history in the dimension of historicity.

In his last days, in the first decade of this century, Henry Adams expressed the hope that on his one-hundredth anniversary he would be permitted a return to the world for a holiday. He cherished the expectation that he "would find a world that sensitive and timid natures could regard without a shudder." His centennial

[4] Wars are favorite themes of historians. For that reason they cannot be entirely classified as historicity, as Spengler and Toynbee seem to have done. One cannot make the "holes in being" an effective subject of written history. Because of wars, however, positive meanings have accrued. War, as Marxists claim, can be a stage on the way to reconciliation in society. Aside from the major gains of World War II one could cite the independence of India in part payment for participation in the war, and the taste of independence in the Far East where the Japanese unseated colonial rule in favor of native rule. Whether a world war can ever again be said to have anything healing in it is a question for which military science in our time is providing a completely new basis for decision.

was the year 1938. Historicity is the shudder the historian feels as he remembers National Socialism and Napoleon. Historicity is the fragments of barbed wire and concrete bunkers which still snag shepherds' cloaks in the fields of Northern France. Historicity is war monuments where the story is preserved of the improvement in bronze seen in plaques successively recording the periodic exhaustion of male populations, as if the human race were in the grip of some demonic almanac. Historicity is the chipped noses of saints in protestantized and republicanized cathedrals, the memory of man's inability to translate, interpret, and otherwise pass smoothly from one epoch to another. Historicity is the pathetic leering images of peasants under cathedral waterspouts conserving the memory of torrents of oppression. Historicity is mutinous mass murder which devours the hand of its own liberator. When history paints the body of the world we live in, it is not an indifferent body, like a Degas dancer or the bucolic women of Renoir. It is the prostitutes of Toulouse-Lautrec—living, human bodies with a presence. But like the bodies of Lautrec, like Lautrec's own, the body of history carries upon it the prophecy of its decay. Historicity is the revelation that the world is, as Gabriel Marcel has called it, *Un Monde Cassé*—like a watch which seems on its surface to tell the time correctly but from which, when held to the ear, one hears *nothing*. History records these corpses of meaning. History is King Lear bearing the tragic body of his daughter. Historicity is Kent, her husband, crying out, "Is this the promised end?"

> Here ends his pleasing dream, his delusive rest, his false peace, his vain security. His joy now vanishes as a cloud; pleasures, once loved, delight no more. They pall upon the taste: He loathes the nauseous sweet; he is weary to bear them. The shadows of happiness flee away, and sink into oblivion: So that he is stripped of all, and wanders to and fro, seeking rest, but finding none.
>
> The fumes of those opiates being now dispelled, he feels the anguish of a wounded spirit. . . . Sometimes it may

> even border upon distraction, making a man "drunken though not with wine," suspending the exercise of the memory, of the understanding, of all the natural faculties. Sometimes it may approach to the very brink of despair; so that he who trembles at the name of death, may yet be ready to plunge into it every moment, to "choose strangling rather than life." Well may such a man roar, like him of old, for the very disquietness of his heart. Well may he cry out, "The spirit of a man may sustain his infirmities; but a wounded spirit who can bear?"[5]

Stephen Dedalus in James Joyce's *Ulysses* summarizes the dimension of historicity in history quite tersely: "History . . . is a nightmare from which I am trying to awake."

A. THE RATIONALITY OF HISTORICITY

How is the rationality of history and therefore of an historical faith affected by the threats of meaninglessness which historicity poses within history? The effect can be observed instructively in the transfiguration which the familiar categories of historical understanding undergo in the dimension of historicity.

Time as Transience. In nature time is always past. It is reality caught at the temporal distance which acts of measurement interpose. In history time is lived, and therefore always present, but lived in the sense of meaningful life. Therefore time is a present extended by the durability of the meanings to which it relates. Historicity is an attack of meaninglessness in which presence is threatened with transience. Transience, then, is the time of historicity, "lost time," the time to which the New Testament refers as "having no hope" (Ephesians 2:12).

Henri Bergson believed the common man's view of time was the time of nature, time fragmented and exteriorized by the human habit of measuring by spaces, as one does on the face of a watch.

[5] John Wesley, Sermon IX, "The Spirit of Bondage and Adoption," *The Works of John Wesley*, Vol. V, Zondervan, pp. 103, 104. In this passage Wesley is characterizing life "under law."

He therefore believed it imperative to help men recover the profounder dimension of lived time, which is an uninterrupted presence, an immersion in the stream of life. Just when theologians and philosophers had accommodated themselves to this transition from natural to historical time, Martin Heidegger articulated a theory of time as transience. Transience is life-time—the time of being-toward-death. He contended that this category of time and not the time of nature was the common man's sense of time. Natural time, the time of spatial measuring, interrupts the flow of lived time with questions which have only a nuisance value to history and tend to trivialize the historical consciousness. The merit of Heidegger's position is to have uncovered a dimension of time which interrupts the flow of lived time with a deepening of the historical question.[6]

Memory as Anachronism. In nature memory is self-forgetfulness in the interests of objectivity. In history memory is self-recollection in the interests of a liaison with the external world of a sort which will confer meaning. In historicity, memory is anachronism. Anachronism is the inability to forget the past. As Thomas Hardy has said, "It may be argued with great plausibility that reminiscence is less an endowment than a disease."

[6] This emphasis was characteristic of Heidegger's earlier writing, preeminently *Sein und Zeit*, where he was preoccupied with the contribution of concrete existence to a knowledge of being. His later writing seems to have reversed this sequence, reading existence in the light of being. *Zeit und Sein* would conceivably be his title for the collection of these essays which have been coming out in this post-World War II period. The result for theologians who are attentive to the theological uses of philosophy is diverting. Rudolf Bultmann and his followers found the earlier Heidegger useful and drew the wrath of the Barthians. Now the Barthians are being wooed by the later Heidegger. See especially Heinrich Ott, *Denken und Sein*, Der Weg Martin Heideggers und der Weg der Theologie, Zurich, 1959. For a full account of this development see *The Later Heidegger and Theology*, a critical discussion by a group of American theologians, edited by James Robinson and John Cobb, Harper, 1963. See also the profound treatment of the theme of time by the Japanese theologian, Seiichi Hatano, *Time and Eternity*, now available in English through the translation by Ichiro Suzuki, published by UNESCO.

Anachronism is reminiscence which blocks self-recollection, like a family which keeps its good habits but has lost its reason for living.[7] This inability expresses itself as guilt. Guilt is not primarily a legal concept, then. For guilt is existence in historicity where one clings to the past long after it has demonstrated its inability to give him a presence. Guilt manifests itself subjectively in the psychological oppressiveness of attempting to carry out historical projects which history does not endorse. It manifests itself objectively in the collapse of these projects.

Language as Misology. In nature language is representational, capturing the movements of the world outside man in a syntax which is the structure of nature. In history language is presentational, recreating the history in which it participates. Historicity, however, sponsors misology, which is a kind of mistrust or even hatred of language. Historicity, which attacks the ability of history to generate a presence, at the same time attacks the power of language to create. This scepticism toward language is not the traditional scepticism based on the dualism between being (the reality) and thinking (the language). It is scepticism based on the impotence of language to provide a history. Written history seems to historicity figures drawn in sand. Every wave of meaninglessness threatens to erase them. As for the language in which its own historical dimension is expressed, the case is no more flattering to language. The language of historicity, like existential language in general, is emotive, composed of sounds of despair and disillusion. These sounds are accurately descriptive of a time of transience and deserve a place in the logic of language. What can a man say when he senses himself falling into the abyss of meaninglessness to the very edge of which he has been tricked unawares by the promise of meaning in history? The vocables of anger or resentment, fear or grief, panic or disillusionment are not ac-

[7] Leni's judgment on her household in Jean-Paul Sartre's *Les Séquestrés d'Altona,* Act I, Scene 1. Sartre perceptively defines this historical sickness as a sickness unto death. "Man is dead," says Frantz, a member of the same family, "and I am his witness." Act II, Scene 1.

credited in standard grammar and syntax. Yet they correspond reliably to the condition of transience. They resemble the sounds one makes when he has lost in love, failed an examination, had a manuscript rejected, tripped on the bottom stair. Historical contingencies and ambiguities can be articulated in standard speech. Historical meaninglessness, which is an attack on one's possibility of being present to himself, invents its language unreflectively in each hollow situation. The language always sounds the same. Operatic sopranos, therefore, who must die of consumption at the final curtain, can rehearse the sound of transience weeks in advance of its occurrence. When it occurs in real life, however, it is always pitifully unique, like Tolstoy's dying Ivan Ilych who for three days "continued screaming on the letter O" or like Hardy's Bathsheba who, upon discovering in the casket with her husband's lover the baby whose birth killed her, "exhaled in the form of a whispered wail: 'O-h-h!'" The grounds for misology here are not that such speech is unclassifiable with standard speech but that it falls too short of representing the true condition it is called upon to signalize. The more positive emotions of love and hope have no such scepticism toward language. If a lover says his words are inadequate, he is engaging in conventional hyperbole. A transcription of the phrases he has used during acts of love would reveal he has often overcommitted himself. Statements of the negative emotions, however, never do them justice. That is why historicity introduces a strain of misology into the experience of history.

Society as Isolation. In nature, society means little more than a structure of classification. In history, it is a structure of relation such as existence between persons in dialogue exemplifies. Society in historicity is experienced as isolation. Not the isolation of nature, of grains of sand on a beach which are together without either willing or enjoying it. One is not easily persuaded by the preternatural language of Alfred North Whitehead, who has the sands of the beach locked together in a love relation. Isolation in historicity is an aggressively active condition, the disrupting of a reality which can only make sense in relatedness. Society is a house which, divided, cannot stand itself. Historicity is society rendered taciturn by lack of trust in language. Words tend to be emotional explosions with no objective correlates. The only form of dialogue known to society in the disruptiveness of historicity is propaganda. Propaganda is the verbal attempt to exorcize disruptiveness by means of disruptiveness (cf. Luke 11:14-28). Propaganda is social gossip, the use of language motivated by hatred of language because it makes language instrumental to intentions which are not intrinsic to the language. Its results are ultimately disruptive because they manipulate individuals around slogans. Slogans appear to provide a basis for relationship but actually only classify. While classification is a condition adequate for nature, in history it only perpetuates isolation.[8]

Decision as Anxiety. The condition of time and language in historicity leaves a heavy burden on decision. Nature, requiring no decision, is often classified as a realm of necessity where free acts are unknown. History, being a realm of ambiguity, requires judgments which take risks. Historicity, however, puts decision in the position of having to eliminate at the level of action a condition of meaninglessness which time creates and language expresses but which neither contributes to removing. Man in historicity is called upon to decide without advantage of a cogent language. At the very same instant, decision is crippled by moods of anxiety brought on through the transience of historicity. Anxiety either contributes to the paralysis of decision or precipitates premature decision. In either case, the risk of decision in historicity is an anxiety-ridden risk. The question placed before it is the crucial question for history: Where has history to go once it has

[8] Cf. Roger Mehl's poignant account of communication: "The men who have exercised an influence on me are not always the ones with whom I have had communication, and in spite of the beneficent influence which they have been able to have on me, they perhaps have not delivered me from my solitude." *La rencontre d'autrui*, Remarques sur le probléme de la communication, Paris, 1955, p. 25.

tasted its own bitterness, once it has audited its own cry of dereliction?

Power as Implosion. In nature, power is a category signifying force. In history, it is a category signifying freedom. Freedom is the balance which historical intelligence introduces into the mechanical forces of nature, giving them such controlled effectiveness that history can conceivably dominate nature. Historicity, on the other hand, is an exposure of historical impotence. The *tetanus* of history which is manifested in forms of historical paralysis is not a sign of the absence of power, however, but of the neutralizing of power. Power in historicity exists in a state of "implosion," where the forces of history are turned against each other. In atomic physics, which invented the term, implosion is the preface to explosion. Analogically, the neutralizing of force in history by balances of power is fraught with implications for historical disruptiveness. Even dreams may shape events into apparently tranquil forms. If the dreams have no relation to durable historical meanings, however, they simply foment disruption.

B. HISTORICITY, THE TINDER OF SIN

Historicity is not evil. It is merely the occasion for human efforts to exist against the intention of history. As such it is a violation of one's humanity brought on by one's humanity, thus not wrong in a simply moral sense, but tragic. That is to say, man's efforts in history are inspired by the meaningfulness of history, yet thwarted by its meaninglessness. This ambivalence is tragic. When the passion to escape the ambivalence becomes inflamed, the situation seems demonic, as if one were not choosing freely but being determined. One can easily see why historians have been fond of the Book of Daniel: it structures history in epochs which successively through God's destination delineate the future, thus lift history out of its potentially tragic ambiguities. The Renaissance, which helped to reveal history as the medium in which man is responsible for working out his own destiny, free from the agency of supernatural powers, discredited the use of the Book of Daniel in historiography. Without such aids to reflection historians have been up against it to see in history what it is that blocks man's capacity to realize himself. The sixteenth-century French historian, Jean Bodin, wrote a book on demonology. In the seventeenth century Bossuet wrote on concupiscence. In the nineteenth century Michelet wrote on satanism and witchcraft. Arnold Toynbee's contemporary analysis of the collapse of cultures is a sophisticated version of the same theme.

The Christian doctrine of original sin is an historiographical insight closer to the Renaissance than to either Daniel or demonology, for it is conceivable in purely historical terms, being based upon the collision of historicity with history. Something is in history which tempts man with hopes which history does not allow him to fulfill. This ambivalence of hope and hopelessness is productive of a tragic situation, in consequence of which one leaps to solutions which violate the intention of history. Nineteenth-century idealists such as Schelling, and Tillich after them, are misleading when they say that the fall of man and not creation is the beginning of history. The fall cannot explain history because history is needed to explain the fall. The transience of history is the tinder of sin, the *fomes peccati.* There man's rejection of his responsibility within the conditions of history can be accounted for. Schelling and Tillich have believed that it is the act of rebellion against God where man first achieves his freedom, and that this freedom is thereafter the source of history. The value of this position was its way of taking seriously the traditional doctrine of original sin without perpetuating the genetic, nature categories in which it was traditionally expressed. Kierkegaard made a significant improvement on this explanation, however, when he proposed that it is in the act of *receiving* God's command, not in the act of revolt against it, that man experiences his freedom and thus the source of his history. The fall away from God is not a willful desire to act on one's own initiative but the sheer drunkenness of anxiety over one's sense of history, of freedom, of possibility. One falls into sin as one falls through inebriation. Kierkegaard therefore conserves a tragic dimension not present in Schelling's view. In the absence of tragic categories, one imports the more explanatory, less historical imagery of demonology, as Tillich does.

Man is an historical being by creation and not by rebellion. His rebellion is accounted for by his history, which is the simultaneous experience of the hope for a meaningful existence (the promise of history) and the sense of its hopelessness (the poverty of history). What he does in that ambivalence will be what determines his existence. Because he does it in ambivalence, it is an anxious act. Because it is an anxious act, it is as if he had not done it but had been the victim. That is why in history it is important to have disclosures of these historical mechanisms to account, as demonologies once did, for this sense that we are falling unaccountably, and by these disclosures regain our equilibrium. The rationality of these disclosures, however, is of the subtlest variety. Not only is it other than the rationality of nature. It is deeper than the ordinary rationality of history. Pascal, himself a tragic thinker, appreciated this subtlety when he said of the doctrine of original sin, "Man is more mysterious without this mystery than the mystery is mysterious to man."

C. A-HISTORICAL SOLUTIONS TO HISTORICAL IRRATIONALITY

The acknowledgment of historicity as the threat of meaninglessness within history itself is therefore a kind of rationality of irrationality. It is a logic of meaninglessness. The formulation is an excessively paradoxical way of saying that history, which is constituted by meaningful life, also embraces a strain of aggressive meaninglessness. Part of the problem for an historical reality like man is finding a way to cope with meaninglessness without leaping out of the historical structure of meaning. The most popular temptations which contemporary culture offers are variations on the method of leaping out of history.

One method of coping with historicity is *positivism*, the joyful, total surrender of all reality to the structure of nature. When the modern mentality insists on "sticking to the facts" it is in danger or reenacting the attitude Oedipus' wife expressed toward tragic truths: "Such things must be forgotten if life is to be endured." Natural sciences address themselves to the facts by vocation and the method of arriving at the facts includes self-forgetfulness. But when a culture lets its whole strategy of life be limited to the realm of facts and engages in universal self-forgetfulness it reveals an anxiety reaction to the terror of history. The French critic, Huysmans, good friend of Cézanne, noticing that the artist excluded human factors from his canvases, accused him of having "a sick retina." Studies in abnormal psychology have shown that the spiritually anxious lack the capacity to interpret facts but will compile them industriously, a phenomenon which has led Merleau-Ponty to observe that "the sick like the learned" verify their hypotheses by assembling facts.[9] Traditionalism in religion participates in the tactic of positivism for the same anxious reasons. Traditionalism derives its strength from the weakness one senses in historical life. Fatigued and perplexed by efforts to cope with historical ambiguities, one is ready to accept the invitation to "return to the faith of the fathers." This faith is seldom the wild, vigorous, prophetic understanding in which most faiths originate but the cautious, secure conservation of things past. When transience challenges presence, the past seems inviting. When historicity threatens history, nature seems a refuge.

Another method of coping with historicity is what Albert Camus proposed as *revolt*. This is the attitude which heroically rejects the meaninglessness of history without objectively affecting the conditions of meaninglessness. Thus, while it does not leap out of history, it exists in a contracted form of history. It interprets history, sees and denies its meaninglessness, but does not change it. Thomas Wolfe was a particularly effective spokesman for this

[9] *Phénoménologie de la Perception*, Paris, 1945, p. 152.

line. In one of his late letters to "Fox" he wrote, "Man was born to live, to suffer, and to die, and what befalls him is a tragic lot. There is no denying this in the final end. *But we must, dear Fox, deny it all along the way.*"[10] One can especially sympathize with the strategy of denial when it occurs in epochs where the element of historicity looms as insuperable. Under such conditions one seems able to survive in history only on the basis of rejection of meaninglessness, although without the possibility of overcoming it. In chains one keeps his sanity by saying "no." In prison one salvages remnants of freedom by chanting, "I am free!" In history one finds meaning in denouncing stupidities he cannot escape. Hester Prynne, who submits to the mores of puritan New England, embroiders her scarlet letter so artistically it could as well stand for achievement as for adultery. Anouilh's *Antigone* helped the French through the German occupation by one simple line in his play, "I am here to say 'no'." Christopher Loque attempted to renew the sentiment for the British in a world threatened by communism when he had the Antigone of his *Trials* say, "I will not share a world with you." Jean-Paul Sartre once counseled Frenchmen not to *abstain* from voting upon de Gaulle's policies because the best way of refusing Machiavellianism is to say "No!" Camus' *Rebel* had already tutored modern man in that procedure. Merleau-Ponty tended to make a permanent program of this *in extremis* method by promoting the view that there is no meaning in history except that which comes from the elimination of non-meaning.[11] Revolt as a permanent policy is an excellent defense against all forms of dogmatism. It is basically a-historical, however, without a positive program of meaning.

The most thoroughly historical among the a-historical solutions to the problem of historicity is *relativism*. "Relativism" here is given only one of the four current connotations of the term, the one that makes relativism most thoroughgoing. For instance, there

[10] Cited by Maxwell Geismar, editor, *The Portable Thomas Wolfe*, Viking, 1946, p. 25.

[11] *Les Aventures de la Dialectique*, Paris, 14th edition, 1955, p. 55.

is perceptual relativism, which can be corrected by the correlation of a multiplicity of observations. There is the relativism which Einsteinian relativity introduced, which accepts the perspective of the observer as an essential part of the data. Like perceptual relativism, this can be objectified through what is known to scientific method as systems of equivalence. There is personal relativism which historians experience who draw different conclusions from the same data, as generals and privates receive different impressions of the same battle. This relativism rejoices that the personal standpoint delivers the historian from what Droysen called an "emasculated objectivism." But it underestimates the extent to which the personal standpoint biases judgment and the importance of correcting this bias by the method the phenomenologists call *epoché* or suspension of judgment.[12]

The fourth kind of relativism, however, seems incurable and is the chief contributor to the sense of historicity in history, for it is the awareness of contingency in history, the consciousness that nothing there is final, ultimate, or enduring. It is the sense of slipperiness in a world in which a man likes to feel something that holds (Herman Melville). The historical method known as relativism adopts this slipperiness as a permanent position. To do so is refreshingly historical in two senses. In the first place, it does not flee from history for its rescue; and in the second, it quite prophetically denies to anyone else the luxury of settling down at any point in history which is not the last word.[13] But when relativists allow the permanent need for attack on false absolutes to become their answer to the problem of meaninglessness in life, they are engaging in a very agile form of distraction which ultimately leaves the problem unsolved. Merleau-Ponty, in approving this strategy of relativism, perceptively characterized it as "a

[12] These three types are briefly discussed by Raymond Aron, *Introduction to the Philosophy of History*, Beacon Press, 1961, pp. 288, 289. Cf. also Morton G. White, *Social Thought in America*, Viking, 1952, Chapter XIV.

[13] See Aron's critique of political messianism and political conservatism, "Histoire et Politique," *Revue de Métaphysique et de Morale*, 1949, pp. 392-407.

movement which leads back and forth between knowledge and ignorance, achieving a kind of repose in the movement."[14]

Philosophy of history, another alternative to historicity, is an effort to anticipate the future on the basis of the experience of the past. In its pessimistic expressions it does not solve the problem of historicity because it adopts historicity as the basic form which history can be expected to take. That is to say, it affirms the ultimate hopelessness of history. But even when it anticipates a future of hope, it does not do so historically. The hopes of history are promises; the hopes of philosophy of history are predictions. The former has a solid root in history which the latter does not claim. History's judgments are portraits which indicate namable events or epochs. Philosophy of history also portrays history, but its portraits are concerned with elaborating types, hence philosophy of history is somewhat indifferent to its living models.[15] The solution which philosophy of history gives to the predicaments of history is suggested by history but not contained in history. In that sense, philosophy of history is a-historical. That is not to deny its influence upon historical life. The success of philosophy of history seems reminiscent of the young governess in Henry James' *The Turn of the Screw.* She was able to satisfy her household that the erratic behavior of her wards was due to ghosts in the house. Luigi Pirandello makes this possibility a major basis for his drama. In *Each Has His Truth,* two characters possess utterly different explanations for the same phenomenon, yet each remains satisfied.

> They have imagined a fiction which has the same consistency as reality and they live therefore in perfect accord, reconciled in this idea. . . . Side by side you have before you fiction on the one hand and reality on the other, and you are incapable of distinguishing them. . . . All that, my dear, is from philosophy.

[14] *Eloge de la Philosophie,* Paris, 1943, p. 11.

[15] Cf. my discussion of philosophy of history in *The Hinge of History,* Scribners, 1959, pp. 34, 35.

The most popular and deceptive trans-historical method in our time for resolving the predicament of history is ontology, or *meta-history*. Meta-history converts historical poverty into a symbol of ontological affluence. It has its source in Hegel. According to Hegel, one who sees the contradictions in history must already be standing at a point beyond them.[16] This deduction is a purely formal claim and, as such, an inversion of the ontological proof for God's existence, a proof which Kant had already discredited. The proof for God moved from the *thought* about a perfect being to the postulate of his existence. This was a leap from the theoretical to the actual, a procedure no more supportable than buying real products with imagined dollars. Hegel, on the other hand, moved from actual historical contradiction to its theoretical resolution, fully as formal a solution as the ontological proof for God, leaving the actualities unchanged. In the case of considerations where a concrete course of inquiry is involved, formal solutions are always sterile.[17] It was Marx who said against Hegel, we must change the world, not merely interpret it. Yet Marx himself proceeded to assign the world a theoretical end which, being far beyond the present in achievability, has put a strain upon his apologists to vindicate in theory what they cannot realize in practice. Wilhelm Dilthey, also instructed by Hegel, realized the limits of history. Like Hegel he saw in the consciousness of limitation the last step in one's liberation from it. Unlike Hegel and Marx he turned to the past rather than the future, the achieved rather

[16] "To be conscious of its own distraught and torn condition and to express itself accordingly—this is to pour scornful laughter on existence, on the confusion pervading the whole and on itself as well: it is at the same time this whole confusion dying away and yet apprehending itself to be doing so." *Phenomenology of Mind*, Baillie translation, p. 546.

[17] This line from a Joseph Conrad letter is a decisive reproof to the method of offering formal solutions for actual predicaments: "What makes mankind tragic is not that they are victims of nature, it is that they are conscious of it. . . . As soon as you know of your slavery, the pain, the anger, the strife—the tragedy begins." Cited by Richard B. Sewall, *The Vision of Tragedy*, Yale University Press, 1959, p. 127.

than the theoretical, for a clue to the overcoming of the limits of history, yet never succeeded in finding there a way beyond these limits.

Heidegger, Jaspers, and Tillich, however, unlike Marx and Dilthey, all depend on Hegel in finding in man, as a temporal and limited being, a breach through which the unlimited reveals itself. In so doing, they show some lack of interest in man in himself, in history in itself. They do not enjoy history as their ultimate destiny but as a symbol of what is at the horizon of history. These contemporary idealistic existentialists are right-wing Hegelians who believe that revelation is possible because history has a lack of reason in it. Contemporary materialistic existentialists are left-wing Hegelians who believe, as Marx himself once said, that "revolution is possible because history has a lack of reason in it." Both wings project man out of the transience which cripples the present into a future which is already in some way promised in the transience. The strength of this position is in the way it follows Hegel in making the future the primary temporal category of history, thus resolving the historical problem of historicity into some form of eschatology. The weakness is in the way this future separates itself from history and pulls the attention of man away from the mainly historical concerns.

The crux of the problem with these popular and influential "meta-historians" is whether the question of meaning in history may not be asked and answered without resort to the science of being, to ontology. Meta-historians make the being-question basic to every *real* question for the formal, logical reason that something can only *be* a question if it in some sense really *is*. Therefore one must necessarily address himself to the *is*-ness, which is ontology. This is a purely formal solution to an existential question, and camouflages an unannounced leap from one genus to another. Marx criticized this meta-historical leap when he defined alienation as an historical problem and insisted on solving the problem as revolutionaries do, rather than as ontologists do. Sartre defied meta-history when he defined man's consciousness not as being but as non-being, that is, as an act of the negation of being. By that turn he subordinated ontology to meontology. Merleau-Ponty has outflanked the ontological being/non-being duality by giving priority to the thoroughly historical meaning/non-meaning (*sens et non-sens*) duality. Martin Werner, the Swiss church historian, is convinced that the issue facing the primitive church was precisely that between the being-question and the question of eschatological meaning. The question of being came to prevail in Christendom, through the influence of Greek philosophy, until the Protestant reformers restored the question of eschatological meaning to the center. The being-question has continued to overshadow the historical question even in Protestantism, however, and Werner believes "the Protestant way" for the future is to gain acceptance of its dominantly historical reading of primitive Christianity. In this context it is misleading for Gerhard Ebeling to say that because theology deals with "all reality," it must undertake ontology.[18] If the reality of the world man lives in is historical, there is no way of going deeper than this reality without slighting the world man lives in.

The ontology of meta-history is enough different from classical ontology that the former cannot be dismissed along with the latter. In classical thinking being was, as Hegel showed, a mere *is* in which man was oblivious of his own being. In the current ontology, being (*Sein*) is self-conscious-being (*Selbstbewusstsein*). In classical ontology being was accessible to thought. In present day ontology being is inaccessible to thought, like the God of the mystics. This aspect is what woos Heinrich Ott, the young Swiss theologian, to Heidegger's ontology. According to Ott, Barth's famous objection that the analogical ontology of Scholasticism is anti-Christ would not be applicable to Heidegger's existential ontology.[19] Most seductive of all is the claim in Heidegger that being is the horizon within which all history happens, apparently making being and history inseparable, while giving being priority.

[18] *Wort und Glaube*, p. 201.
[19] *Denken und Sein*, pp. 29, 30.

What Heidegger says of the being of history, however, Plato had already said. It is the moving image of eternity. Unlike Plato, Heidegger is a phenomenological ontologist: being never "appears" except in human being, in history. But when it appears, it appears as being and not as man, as being and not as meaning, as "the sound of the silence" which is "nothing human," therefore not as history.[20] To that extent, like Plato, Heidegger can visualize eternity in distinction from its moving image. To say being is the horizon, the destiny, the limit of history is, indeed, to say that being is the "historicity of history" (Max Müller). Being puts history in crisis as its ultimate source and possibility. Hence one can legitimately talk, as Heidegger does, of an "eschatology of being." This ontological eschatology, however, does not put history in question in the same way Christian eschatology does, entirely as history. That is why the apparently historical character of the ontology must be regarded rather as a meta-history, a way of being which is less than completely historical. As Paul Ricoeur has noticed, "Heidegger wrote *Sein und Zeit* without a single reference to the European crisis and in an ontological horizon closer to Parmenides than to the contemporary public consciousness."[21] His later writings show even less awareness of history. To make the question of "being," which is the ontological question, prior to the question of "meaning," which is the historical question, is to assume that philosophers and theologians can do more than *exist* in their formulations. If one exists where he thinks, history has primacy over all other methods of reflection, even over ontology. Existence is not a symbol of being but the final medium of man's life. To forget that is to forget what Dilthey meant when he said, "Man is there not to be but to act."[22]

[20] *Unterwegs zur Sprache*, p. 30.

[21] *Histoire et Vérité*, Paris, 1955, p. 246.

[22] *Gesammelte Schriften*, Vol. V, p. xv. My critique of "the later Heidegger" has been elaborated in an essay, "Theology as Ontology and as History," in the volume *The Later Heidegger and Theology*, Robinson and Cobb, editors.

II. ESCHATOLOGY AS HISTORICAL FINALITY

The historical significance of the Christian faith is to be found in the way in which, in its eschatology, it reveals the finality of history. Like eschatologies in general, it announces the end of history. The end it announces is the end of the wretchedness in which historical obscurity forces men to live. The form in which the end is announced is Jesus of Nazareth, an historical figure. The form in which the end is realized is the Kingdom of God, the configuration of human relations where God's purpose as manifest in Jesus of Nazareth becomes the mode of man's existence in the world. The form in which the historical transition is made between the announcement of the end and its realization is the church, the body in which history is responsible for overcoming its meaninglessness in virtue of the end of history. Jesus founded the church as a means to the Kingdom of God. The church thereafter lives by losing its life as means in order that the end of history may be fully achieved. The existence of the church is both the hope of the achievement of the Kingdom of God and the sign of its inachievement. The withering away of the church will be the sign of the achievement of the Kingdom only if human history is at that time enjoying transparency toward its end.

"End of history" is a notoriously ambiguous phrase. In the Christian eschatology it cannot mean that history is "terminated," except in the specialized sense that the presence of Jesus of Nazareth in history put an end to history in its old form. It cannot mean history is "completed," except in the sense that in the full obedience of Christ, and intermittently of the saints of the church, the rule of God has been fully present. "End of history" in the Christian eschatology signifies the permanent meaning communicated by the event of Jesus of Nazareth, because that event overcomes historicity by vitiating the obscurity of history. The continuance of history after the death of Jesus was not a refutation of his role in bringing the end, as Albert Schweitzer and his followers mistakenly contend. The fact that the world has not ceased to run since Christ announced its end does not mean that Christ was wrong about the end but that some were wrong about what he meant by "end." Jesus appeared not as the enemy of the actual movement of history but as its redeemer. Himself a fully historical person, his obedience to God in calling the world to obedience supplies the conditions within which history may overcome the anxiety of its own inherent meaninglessness. He is, as St. Augustine called him, "the end without end."

A. MATURITY IN THE WORLD

How does one arrive at this astonishing dilation of a single otherwise diminutive historical moment? In the same way one arrives at the knowledge of any historical event. In the same way Jesus himself arrived at that knowledge. Jesus of Nazareth was born into a human world, a world of "polished wood and stone tortured . . . into shapes" by all before and around him. That world, as every historical world, was an invitation to decipher its meaning and then reshape it. A circuit of understanding waits to be completed in every historical existence. In the face of the events of our lived world, which are heavy with the meanings stamped upon them, one is called upon to make his own interpretation. Considering the spirit of the interlocutor which animates each historical being, man cannot help but ask the meaning of events from deep within his own concern. With these ingredients and within these conditions Jesus hazarded a judgment about himself, as all who live in history hazard. "Are you he who was to come, or look we for another?" That was the question his time posed to him, the question he posed to himself, and the question through which we continue today to make him our contemporary. Jesus' conclusions about himself have subsequently shaped our world as they did the world of his own time. Through his apostles and through the mediation of the historical community which lives by its memory of him, we are invoked to repeat the interpretive cycle. Our conclusions will determine whether the end he brought will find its consummation in our history. Yet, like history in general, our conclusions will be influenced by his world of polished wood and stone tortured into a shape which keeps his memory endlessly alive for us.

What then is the meaning of the event which shapes our history cruciform, then waits to be deciphered? Why are the words so final which Jesus spoke in saying, "It is finished"? What is its eschatological significance, its meaning as end of history? Jesus is the end of history because he was "faithful unto death" in obedience to God. The content of his obedience was that he read himself as the one in whom God had chosen to call the world to obedience. One who obeys the implications in Christ's obedience will anchor himself firmly in history, that is, assume the responsibility for shaping a world. In Jesus of Nazareth such responsibility is revealed to be the meaning of history. One can now judge history from an end that is present, no longer living with a wistfulness that carries one out of the medium made for men. The purposes of God are now explicit at one point in history. That means all divinization of nature and history is terminated. No gods are to be looked for anywhere. Nothing has been changed in the world by that event except everything that matters most to men and God—the meaning of the world. God through the faithful ministry of Jesus of Nazareth has turned the world over to men. As the Apostle Paul told the Galatians, "You are no longer a slave but a son, and if a son then an heir" (Galatians 4:7). In this event the intention of creation is radically fulfilled: henceforth man is to subdue the earth.

Dietrich Bonhoeffer suggested in posthumously published fragments that the church needs to recognize the maturity of modern man. Modern man has "come of age." He must therefore be treated as an adult, not as a child. He need not be reduced to sackcloth and ashes before being recruited for Christian discipleship. God chooses to use men in their strength and not to make them weak. Another German theologian, Friedrich Gogarten, has contended in a more voluminous literature that the maturity of man is not primarily an achievement of the modern world but the direct fruition of the ministry of Jesus of Nazareth. Because of Jesus man is "a child of God." To be a child of God is an historical and not a genetic, natural form of existence. To be a "child of God" is not the substance of the human nature but the possibility in history which Jesus' announcement of the end of history commences. To be "a child of God" is to be set within an historical framework in which one begins to assume his responsibility for a world which God has turned over to him.[23]

The concept of a man "come of age" is an eighteenth-century formula. In his essay, "What is Enlightenment?", Kant defined the age of the Enlightenment as "the world of the man come of age." The sense of man's power over the world—in responsibility though not in fact—had already flowered in Renaissance times and has continued up to this moment. Chateaubriand noticed it when he saw the decline of monarchies and the emergence of democracies. "Now that nations have come of age," he said, "they claim they no longer need a tutor." Sorel noticed it when he realized that artists work with no sense of the need for a reward in an after-life. Why then do men need ends beyond history as incentives for responsibility in history? Nietzsche expressed the same when he had Zarathustra console the dying "rope dancer" after his fatal fall from the tightrope in mid-act, "There is no devil and no hell." When the dying man replied that in such a case he must be like an animal who would lose nothing by losing his life, Zarathustra moved the man to gratitude by showing him that he was simply to die as he had lived: "Thou hast made danger thy calling. . . . Now thou perishest by thy calling." Richard Rothe, nineteenth-century German moralist, saw the same drive in Christianity when he visualized maturity of history expressing itself in an arrangement where the functions of the church would one day

[23] See the brief essay on Gogarten's view of secularization by L. E. Shiner in *Motive* magazine for May, 1962; also, the forthcoming presentation of Gogarten's theology by Theodore Runyon, Jr., in a work on contemporary theologians to be published by Meridian Press, Marvin Halvorsen, editor.

be assumed by the people as a whole. What may sound like a terrifying piece of Prussianism is really a simple exegesis of the scriptures. Karl Barth has virtually said the same. "The object of the promise and the hope in which the Christian community has its goal consists, according to the unmistakable assertion of the New Testament, not in an eternal church but in the *polis* built by God and coming down from heaven to earth."[24] That analysis, historically interpreted, would mean that one day the church not only must accept the state from God—as it now does. One day the church must allow itself to be dissolved in a mature state.

The modern intimation of what the end of history means had already occurred to the reformers. Calvin and Luther wrote no commentaries on the Book of the Revelation. That book had been captured by "fanatics" who either projected human life beyond history, depleting responsibility toward history, or chose to define responsibility in the world as rejection of the world through martyrdom. Calvin preached of election, which meant for man the explication of his divine calling through concrete historical activity. Luther preached of justification by faith alone, which meant that man could let the world be a world because he need not exploit it as a means to salvation beyond the world. The medieval church had realized this dimension of faith when it

[24] Karl Barth, *Community, State and Church,* Three Essays by Karl Barth, with an introduction by Will Herberg, Anchor Book, p. 154. In the same essay, "Christian Community and Church Community," p. 157, Barth nevertheless rejects Rothe's proposed absorption of the church by the state on the grounds that it would be against the welfare of the state, for it would mean the gospel would not be proclaimed. States do not preach or pray. Therefore the state would lose its most valuable critic. This is no real criticism of Rothe not simply because Rothe's proposal is predicated upon a maturity not conceded in Barth's essay, but because under the conditions of maturity described, one would continue to receive the state from God, a posture which cuts across the tyranny and injustice potential in states and without which the *polis* would fall apart again into a dialectic of church and state. Rothe's position is more dialectical than the position of Thomas Hobbes, a viewpoint not without its unwitting adherents among present-day Christians. In his *Leviathan,* Hobbes indicated

depicted Christ on his cross as a victor on a throne, himself the first fruits of the new man heralded in his announcement of the Kingdom of God. The achievement of Dante was that he allegorized the rest of the whole crude mechanism of medieval other-worldliness. In his travel through hell, purgatory and paradise he never leaves the world. He wishes to say that the Christian faith is the history of the life of man; through revelations of the self-defeating ambiguities of this world, man is being brought nearer to God. Like a medieval Prometheus, Dante translated the fires of inferno into a spiritual pilgrimage which man lives out in this world.[25] Irenaeus had already provided the pattern for this historicizing of the drama of salvation. He was strongly under the influence of views of history which had no essential relation to the Christian end. Nevertheless, he saw Jesus of Nazareth as the one who, by his thoroughgoing recapitulation of historical existence, achieved the conditions by which man, the created child, could be brought to maturity, the maturity which God had always had in mind for him.

That, then, is what Jesus chose when he said of himself, "I am the way." Not a badge of exclusiveness, except as the liberating implications of his way cut across worldly procedures designed to keep man living in insecurity or in false security. Rather, Jesus

---

that Christ's purpose was to restore the immortality which Adam lost for the human race. However, that restoration would have to await the last resurrection, when the kingdom is believed by Hobbes to begin. The present would belong to the State. Christians, unlike Marxists, anticipate that history moves not toward a stateless society, an unimaginably utopian situation, but toward a churchless society. Meanwhile, the existence of the church is a limit to remind states that they are not final. The existence of the state is just as much a limit to remind churches that history stands under the judgment of some more inclusive society than their fellowship exemplifies.

[25] For this interpretation of Dante I am primarily indebted to Ernst Troeltsch's reference to K. Voszler, *Die göttliche Komödie* in "Eschatologie," *Religion in Geschichte und Gegenwart*, first edition. A similar point of view more recently expressed can be found in Erich Auerbach, *Mimesis*, Meridian, 1957, pp. 151-177.

of Nazareth is the open door by which the whole of history may live a history of wholeness. Not the datable beginning of a new epoch, but the realization of the truth about God and man which makes all epochs new beginnings. Not the end of physical death but the end of historical death, which is death as the object of man's care, where the question of man's future is at issue. Not the end of sin, but the beginning of the end of sin because the end of the conditions of historical ambivalence which makes men prone to sin. Not the end of law but the end of the bondage to the law as an instrument for vindicating one's right to inherit the world. Not the end of dependence upon God, but the beginning of an existence in which *everything* is received from God, hence under responsibility to him. Therefore, not the end of God in the world but the end of God as the explanation of the world and the beginning of God as the source of the world's meaning.[26]

B. THE LOGIC OF ESCHATOLOGY

I have said one arrives at the knowledge of the end of history as one arrives at any form of historical understanding. That is only partially true. Not all historical events have the same status as history. Some are *originating* (epoch-making) events, like marriages, revolutions, and declarations of independence. Others are *explicative* (epochal) events, the living out of the implications in the special events. While both kinds of event are understood by the same historical methods of interpretation, they do not necessarily retain the identical historical structure. In the Chris-

[26] Merleau-Ponty has perceptively defined the difference between the older atheism and contemporary atheism. The older atheists explained the world without God. The newer atheists find the world inexplicable. *Signes*, Paris, 1960, p. 191. By that distinction one may conclude that Christianity is at odds with the older atheism because that atheism expressed itself within the structure of nature. The newer atheism comes quite close to Christianity in two senses. First, it rejects the use of the idea of God as a tool for explaining the world. Second, it lives with concern for meaning in the world, opening up a sense of lack in history to which a faith can speak.

tian understanding, the event of Jesus of Nazareth emerges as the covenant of God with human history in which a new age, the final age of history's maturity appears, and in which the old age of obscurity and its attendant anxiety is overcome.[27]

The quality of newness, finality, and ultimacy in eschatological history affects the rationality of faith. To say that Christianity is an eschatological faith is to say it is an historical access to maturity in history. It is God's break-through to humanity which shows humanity how it can finally enjoy its life in the world. One need no longer be distracted by religious and philosophical fancies which ask man to trade his relatively certain life in the world for the uncertain hopes of an other than worldly life. One need no longer allow his uneasy conscience to be exploited by latter-day theorists who pose as authorities on the secret counsels of God. To call Jesus of Nazareth the last word in history means to believe that in him God has said what he intends to say. Man can now work out his own salvation by that final word. The first need no longer force themselves to be last or to discipline themselves into self-abasement. For God has called man out of weakness and appealed to him to be strong. The strength which the word of God communicates is not some metaphysical infusion of power such as analogies drawn from technology tempt one to seek. The strength

[27] Cf. the remarkable discussion by Etienne Trocmé showing that the New Testament "historian," the author of Luke-Acts, attempted to imitate the historiography of the pagan world, for apologetic reasons. The effort is judged unsuccessful. Modern historians who think they find a confrere in Luke are naive. The author of Luke-Acts is less an historian than he is a church official with a good memory. He is an amateur historian insufficiently trained for his task. Although Trocmé does not do so, one could draw the conclusion from this failure that the New Testament events did not lend themselves at all to treatment by the nature-oriented historiography of the classical world and did not lend themselves entirely to the form of history in general. The most conspicuous proof of this could be the fact that, as Trocmé himself indicates, both the Gospel of Luke and the Acts of the Apostles "recoil from eschatology." *Le "Livre des Actes" et L'Histoire*, Paris, 1957, p. 39.

is the historical freedom of final purpose which mobilizes all man's worldly forces on behalf of a distinct end.

Obviously the term "eschatology" is not being used here as it has been used traditionally, to refer to "the last things." It is not a study of immortality, the conditions of life after death and the judgment at the terminus of history. As Paul Tillich long ago pointed out in his *Religiöse Verwirklichung, eschata* of this sort lack the ultimacy for inspiring our trust. They are anthropological in focus, tutoring man to think of his end in terms of his condition there rather than in terms of God's presence. Biblical eschatology rather deals with *eschaton*, the last, the ultimate, the final reality, reality as an attribute of God's being present, the promise of God, who alone inspires man's trust. Therefore it is fatuous to assume that eschatology is to the end of things what archaeology is to the beginning of things, as Jean Daniélou once proposed, or to conjecture about eschatology on the basis of scientific or political theories about how the world will be consummated, as Karl Heim has done so seductively.

Christ puts an end to the world. That is what it means that history is eschatological. The Christian faith is *not one religion alongside others*, for it puts an end to religion. Religions search for God and attempt to penetrate his mystery by liturgical and moral practices. In Christ, God is revealed in one word. Christianity, therefore, is *not a mythological faith*, for several reasons: (1) It knows only *one* incarnation of God in human history. Karl Marx once pointed to this as an important difference between the Christian "religion" and religions in general where theophanies tend to proliferate. (2) The conviction that it was God who spoke in Jesus of Nazareth appeals to nothing but history—to an event which is fully human, fully historical. (3) God's word is *heard* in the words of Jesus of Nazareth. Mythology makes God's word an object of historical description. Eschatological faith is non-mythological because it leaves God's word in the form of address, of proclamation, of word. Far from being an object about which one makes up stories, God's word is the subject and source for a whole new mode of history. (4) This event in which God addresses history continually wages war upon mythologies in and outside Christendom by dismissing any necessity to deceive ourselves about finalities in history. Like a poultice absorbing all the poisons of the body, this one word, the word of God in Jesus of Nazareth, exorcises all the quests for finality which leave history wretched with unfulfillment. Christianity is *not a plan of salvation,* for it is the promise of salvation. It puts an end to man's anxieties about his own destiny by announcing that his destiny is complete in the Christ event and that he may now work out that destiny in freedom, without care. Christianity is *not a body of teachings,* for it is response to the word of God the content of which is reducible to very simple terms: "Accept the world from God, make it your responsibility, and do not allow yourself to be enslaved in it again," not even by religion, not even by morality, not even by philosophy. Christianity is *not a preparation for life after death,* for it is a candid admission that we know nothing of such a future except that God is in it, and that we need no other basis in or beyond the world than that confidence in God. Christianity is *not a code of conduct,* for it puts an end to all words but God's word in Christ. He is the only irreplaceable word, for he is the covenant, the person, the speech-event, through whom God gives us the world, and without whom, therefore, the world threatens to engulf us. Christianity tells us nothing we cannot find out for ourselves except that in Christ God has turned the world over to man. If we forget that we receive the world from God, the world will put an end to us. Christianity is *not,* therefore, *a counsel of despair,* as people fear it is where the so-called "last things" of eschatology are elevated to such prominence. Eschatological faith puts an end to despair by giving man a final hope in Christ, a hope which does not reduce one's present stature, but puts the whole responsibility for the world on man; a hope which does not leave man without divine aid, but grants him the power of God in the medium of history, which is the medium in which man becomes free, intelligent, and responsible.

In short, a Christian is one who knows the fruits of the spirit. These fruits are structures of existence, not intellectual data. They are fully historical realities which are lived out in men. Among them are love, joy, peace, patience, kindness, goodness, faithfulness, gentleness, and self-control. These are the attributes of a life of freedom, a life of responsibility prepared for in God's final word to history in Jesus of Nazareth. They are the eschatological attributes. That does not mean one must wait for them until some future time. In Christ as the end of history these attributes are now being prepared in man. Life in Christ realized in these eschatological attributes is the maturity of history. The unknown world will remain unknown, but there will be no more *fear* of the unknown. Sadness will continue to interrupt us, but it will not dominate us. Enmity will continue to corrode us, but it will not destroy us. Anxiety will continue to distract us, but it will not permanently derange us. Our greed will continue to bias us, our infidelities will continue to shame us, our inflated conceit will make us hard and our frustrated conceit will make us overbearing, but not one of these things will engulf us finally because the final word has been spoken and has brought us to maturity, which is the power to overcome the world.

Without taking faith out of history, eschatology nevertheless transvalues historical understanding. This transvaluation can be seen in the startling shift which the historical categories undergo when placed in the eschatological context.[28]

[28] The conviction that the historical "categories" are "transvalued" by "eschatological history" saves my discussion from the judgment of Otto Weber of Göttingen. He has said that there are no "categories" in history by which one can understand the "eschatological event." By that he means what I would wish to say, namely, that existence in "eschatological history" is not a derivative of possibilities in "general history" or even in "existential history." "The self-witness of Jesus has no *a priori* on its side" (*Grundlagen der Dogmatik*, Vol. II, Neukirchen, 1962, pp. 46f. and 111ff.). Cf. my use of Husserl's categoreal viewpoint in Chapter II, note 24. See also Weber's application of the eschatological dimension of history to the problems of Christology (*ibid.*, pp. 97ff.).

Time as Imminence. In eschatological history, the category of time is, as one would expect, future. But eschatological time is future in a highly specialized sense. It is future because it is beyond transience, as the past is not, and is thus capable of granting man a presence. There is a future which has not yet come. That future is deficient in history because the present cannot enter into it. But there is also a future which keeps coming in such a way as to make the present meaningful, notwithstanding the transience of historicity. That is the future as imminence.

The failure to understand the distinction between these two futures divides Christian interpreters today as it divided early Christians. It marks the difference between apocalyptic and eschatology. Apocalyptic projects faith as a hope into a future not yet come. Eschatology grasps what has come decisively in Jesus Christ as a future which continues to come in such a way as to support our present. Theologians have attempted to harmonize these two attitudes because they are both expressed in the New Testament. That hermeneutical attitude is lacking in historical rigor and sensitivity, for it fails to observe what is there for the historical understanding, namely, the element of struggle in the early church for the conservation of a distinctive Christian specification of the end.[29] Jesus of Nazareth came as the end. The apocalyptic Judaism of his time influenced some of his followers to believe that if he were the end, he must return to the world again, for the end had not yet come. This position was a curious denial of the radical character of the Christ event. It has suc-

[29] For this reason I believe Raymond Aron is wrong to say that the dialectic between tradition and freedom is one of the three most important elements in the historical consciousness. (*Dimensions de la conscience historique*, Paris, 1961, p. 95.) It need not be the task of the historical consciousness to break with a tradition as if it were a fate, for tradition has within it its own dialectic, its own self-critical process, its own method of purification. As the Japanese theologian, Yoshitaka Kumano, has shown, tradition is a reality embracing both *dento* and *densho*, both tradition as conservation and tradition as active, history-producing witness. The task of the historian is to let the vital tradition *liberate itself* from the dead weight of tradition.

ceeded in dominating the thought of the church through sheer terminological confusion. The apostolic witness conserves a record not of equally acceptable alternative views of the end, and not at all of reconcilable alternatives, but of the struggle of the Christian faith for its radicality. Projection of hopes into the chronological future is the quickest way to neutralize a hope. When the sisters of Lazarus said in the presence of Jesus, "I know the Messiah *will come*," they conjugated eschatology in the wrong tense. Jesus is recorded as correcting them: "*Now* is the time." The Gospel of John is an aggressive, almost irritated repetition of "now, now, now" against the efforts to compromise the efficacy of Jesus with a future which had not yet come. "The hour *now* is when the true worshipper will worship the father in spirit and in truth" (4:23). By these words Jesus judged that one who says the Messiah *will* come is not living under the conditions of "spirit and truth." He has neutralized into an indeterminate future the truth which is given for our presence.[30]

Christianity is fundamentally at odds with the seductive eschatologies of both Marxism and existentialism for the same reason that it is at odds with apocalypticism. Marxism projects an apocalyptic future whose fulfillment has not yet come. That is why it can justify reducing the present to a means, a means to distant ends, sacrificing the present to the future. Existentialism defines the future as a mood of expectation within the present toward a future which one can only await. As such, though in a different way, it also sacrifices the present to the future. Christian eschatology, on the other hand, is concerned with a future which confers fulfillment upon the present. *Now* is the time of maturity for

[30] Cf. Ernst Käsemann's description of this struggle over eschatology in the Gospel of Matthew, "Die Anfänge christlicher Theologie," *Zeitschrift für Theologie und Kirche*, Nov., 1960, pp. 162ff.: "Matthew reveals a history filled with the strongest theological tensions." The same can be said for almost any New Testament writing. The task of the interpreter is not to harmonize the tension but to attempt to determine what was at stake for essential Christianity.

the Christian. Now are the Christians filled with the eschatological beatitudes and attributes of spirit. Now the Kingdom of God has begun. One who loses his life in it will find his life not later but *now.*

One might ask why it is any longer legitimate to refer to this end of history as a future at all. Is it not a reality "in the last analysis" which may as well be described as a reality "in the first synthesis"? (I have learned this formulation from the French philosopher, Jean Wahl.) I believe that is actually the case. It would be better not to talk of the Christian future at all than to talk of it as not yet come. The New Testament seems to support this possibility when it refers to Christ as the end who is also the beginning. The importance of identifying this beginning as a future, however, is to separate it from a past which is gone and from a present which fades away under the erosion of transience. Christ is an event primarily future because he is the end of transience and the beginning of a permanent presence. That is to say, the word "future" in Christian thinking about the Christ event signifies the capacity of this event to keep all events under the judgment of the meaning which it brings. As such, Christ is not one in a series of chronological events but the teleological source of a whole mode of existence. When the early church prayed for his coming they did right to say, "Marana tha"—"our Lord, come!" For the verb is expressed in the present imperative, and could very well mean, "Keep on coming!" "O do not set him a time!" plead John Wesley. "Expect him every hour. Now he is nigh! even at the door!" (Sermon VI)

Memory as Forgiveness. The problem of memory in history is its tendency to remember the wrong things. A natural scientist while thinking of himself cannot be responsible to his data. An historian who does not think of himself cannot be responsible to his. A man of the world who cannot forget his past has a closed future. Eschatological faith is the dimension of history in which memory has its end in Jesus of Nazareth. All dimensions of time emanate from one sacramental time, the time of doing "in remembrance of" him, which is the time of forgiveness. When history is embraced by that event, scientists may let their data be, no longer being distracted by preoccupation with themselves. They do not have to "prove" anything. Historians may let themselves be in their data, no longer living in the necessity for self-rejection. The man of the world may be exhilarated by a future he never knew was there, being liberated from the burden of an inadequate past or from unillumined loyalty to effete causes.

Language as Performatory. The language of eschatological history is presentational, as is all historical language. However, it survives the misology and revolt of historicity in a way that other historical language does not. The survival value of the apostolic language prompted the early church to call it the word of God. The word of God is historical language which it not derivable from history in general but rather has the power to create history in the face of the nothingness of historicity. Long ago Plato attempted to redeem the evident weakness of words by letting language be transcended in a voiceless dialogue of ideas. Ever since, Christianity has found it difficult to say what it means that the Word has become flesh. The church has been mystified that what it binds on earth is bound in heaven. Preachers have remained puzzled when their verbal patches on the garment of the Gospel have resisted moths or when the tinkling brass of their homilies has not always rusted away. Now it is known, however, that language is not simply the container of ideas which exist in their own right without that medium. Language is itself the horizon in which life is illuminated, as the morning sun illuminates the landscape.

"My words abide," said Jesus, "for what I say, I say on the authority of my Father in heaven. These words do not perish, for they are the words of eternal life." Where the apostles heard their own witness to Jesus of Nazareth they were moved by the same sense of the durability of their words, the same sense of their creative ability: "We have his message of reconciliation. God now makes his appeal through us." The Christian tradition has called this the language of revelation. No word could have been more ambiguous, for all language is revelational in its own way. The language of nature "reveals" the syntax of the structure of nature as X-ray "reveals" the bony structure of a body. But that is not at all what Christians mean by revelation. The language of history "reveals" the structure of history by actually bearing historical meaning and existing as history incarnated into word, as personal letters and diaries incarnate the lives of their authors, retaining in phrases the power to evoke a presence. Christianity means almost precisely that by revelation. But there is still a difference. The language of eschatology "reveals" a particular presence, the presence of God, the final presence which appears when the word of God in Jesus of Nazareth brings man's life out of potential nothingness into meaningful expression. That language is not simply presentational, like the historical tradition out of which a people continues to build its life. It is "performatory," like the word of God at the creation of the world. I first learned about performatory language from the Oxford analyst, J. L. Austin. Hegel also seems to have known about it. "It is the power of utterance *qua* utterance which, just in speaking, performs what has to be performed."[31] The language of creation is performatory: when God said, "Let there be," "there was." The language of incarnation is performatory: when God incarnated himself in history, he whispered in the ear of Mary. The language of the church is performatory: when the witness proclaims the apostolic faith, he does not set up live options for the auditor's choice; he creates the possibility of that choice.

Compare, then, the possible meanings in this familiar sentence from Pauline eschatology, "All things are yours" (1 Cor. 3:21). It could have any one of three meanings. It could be descriptive, in which case it would mean, "These things belong to you." It could

[31] *Phenomenology of Mind*, Baillie translation, p. 530. The historical interpretation of creation as elaborated in Chapter I of this volume should be kept in mind in sensing the meaning of this analogy from creation to creative language.

name certain objects, in which case it would mean, "These are things which belong to you." For the Apostle, however, it is actually performatory, for it means, "These things are now turned over to you." In that utterance, eschatological language creates a world which did not heretofore exist. Those who hear that word describe themselves as "new creatures in Christ." The content of their newly created life is responsibility for the world which their responsibility to God has evoked.

To call language performatory may seem to classify communication with incantation, unless it is realized that the purpose of historical language is not to point to things but to change situations. In the last century, Horace Bushnell perceptively illuminated this problem of language in theology. Theology deals with the spiritual phenomena of faith, he said. Accessible languages, however, are largely oriented to things. Therefore, theological language has drawn analogies to spiritual reality based on the experience with things. However, one tends to forget the spiritual intention of his language and begins to look for the equivalence to things suggested in his thing-oriented language. When that happens, the language of faith loses its power to change situations. Jonathan Swift in *Gulliver's Travels* proposed to foreign diplomats how, when they cross borders into other countries, they can avoid learning a new language. They need simply carry with them all the objects to which they expect to refer. Instead of speaking, they have only to point.

Some feel that this tactic of pointing is the source of language, so that words become surrogates of things. What does one do, however, if he is not a diplomat but a missionary, and he feels obliged to point to God? A minister may stand before his congregation and use certain special words like "pulpit," "Bible," "layman," or even "God." Is it any special advantage to him that he can point to the pulpit before him as an object, or to the Bible at his side, or to the layman in the pew, if in fact he cannot point to God? In history, there is no special advantage to a language that can point to things, because the purpose of historical language is not to indicate objects but to change situations. Hence when one says "pulpit" he is not pointing to a thing. He is saying, "the world is a ship in its passage out, and the pulpit is the prow of the world" (Herman Melville). When he says "Bible" he is confessing that God has not left himself without a witness. When he says "layman" he is not designating a person who is not a clergyman; he is invoking a way of life:

> Rise up O man of God
> Have done with lesser things.

And when he says "God"? The word "God" is not an invitation to point to some transcendent reality. It is an invocation to receive the world from beyond oneself. "God" when uttered and confessed creates the situation of eschatological history where a man receives everything from beyond himself.

When a man says to his beloved, "I love you!" he is not pointing to his emotional states. He is transforming a situation. When the church says to man, "God loves you," it is not making statements about God's attributes. It is creating a covenantal history. That is why in the Biblical faith, when God "creates" the world, he speaks and there is: something is made out of nothing; when God incarnates himself in Jesus of Nazareth, the word is made flesh: the old age comes to an end, and the new age begins; when God raises Jesus from the dead, the church is given a message: the dead in their trespasses and sins are given an eternal life.

A case can be made for the difference between an Old Testament understanding of "the word" and a New Testament understanding which throws light on the special historical character of an incarnational, eschatological faith. In the incarnational view of the New Testament it is understood that the word not only effects a new situation. What it effects it simultaneously interprets. History since New Testament times is not events which are subsequently in need of interpretation. History is meaningful occurrence: events which confer meaning. Albert Schweitzer once made the provocative observation that Jesus' eschatological position contrasted with that of apocalyptic Judaism because Jesus was the first to attempt to precipitate the advent of the Kingdom of God by a word alone. Other heralds of the kingdom had exploited antecedent catastrophes of one sort or another. Jesus simply came preaching. Yet, by this view Jesus is fully within the line of the Old Testament understanding of the word where the word is believed to effect results, as lightning does, or as a "hammer that breaketh a rock." Origen fell into the same framework when he compared the word of the apostles to the trumpets of Israel at the battle of Jericho. Incarnational language, however, not only effects results. It is historical language because it combines with the effects the motives which can persist in the produced effects. That is why it is important to say that eschatological language, a performatory language, is performatory in a fully historical sense, where events occur in such a way as to confer meaning.[32]

Society as Church. A language which communicates a memory of Jesus of Nazareth as the Christ overcomes the isolation of historicity by creating the eschatological community called the church. The church is eschatological because it is a community formed by the imminent presence of God in his word in Jesus of Nazareth. The church is a community in which human isolation is being overcome through response to the reality of God who has come in such a way as hereafter always to be coming. Like every generally historical society, it knows its existence through and for the sake of meaningful human relationships, and it knows that these relationships are expressible through dialogue. Unlike communities in general, it identifies Jesus of Nazareth as the pivotal person in whom all these communal relationships are mediated into an ultimate relation. It knows that all its conversations center upon the one topic which mediates that relation, the word of

[32] Cf. Ernst Fuchs' discussion of the difference between the Hebrew *dabar* and the Greek *logos* in *Religion in Geschichte und Gegenwart*, third edition, article entitled "Logos." Cf. also Hans-Georg Gadamer, *Wahrheit und Methode*, Tübingen, 1960, p. 397: The greater miracle of speech is not that the word becomes flesh, but that in doing so it nevertheless remains word.

God. Because it hears that eschatological word, it knows itself as a community in which there is real peace, real reconciliation, all the fruits of the spirit in communal form. Because it bears that word, it knows itself not as a privileged but as a responsible community. Because it hears the word as out of the future, in imminence, it knows it can only preach that word as out of the future. That is, not as the inescapable conclusion to a series of facts but always only as a possibility for decision. Because the word is the last word, the church knows it is the community in which God's triumph in history is being realized. But because it is called to be the bearer of that word, the eschatological reality of the church is not in its triumph but in its militancy. Because the effect of its militancy is to make men responsible in the world and not dependent upon the church, it knows its highest moment of triumph will be the moment in which its militancy has succeeded in making of the world a church, that is, in rendering the church as a separate entity superfluous.

Decision as Grace. The decision which eschatological history evokes is different from the decisional character of history in general since it is tied to the particular event in which God gives us the world. Like the decisions of history in general, it is made both in the risk of historical ambiguity and within the conditions of presentational meanings, meanings which solicit and seduce decision. Eschatological decision is only different from the decisions of history in general in respect of a curious simultaneity in which the element of risk is at once both intensified and reduced. The risk is intensified in eschatological decision because the stakes are higher. This decision is a life or death decision. The ultimate meaning of our existence is at stake when we are confronted by an ultimate claim. It is an all or nothing decision, for one cannot will to live *both* under the decisive historical revelation *and* under the conditions that pre-exist that revelation. Hence there is a terrifying element which is a direct attribute of the critical profundity of the moment of decision.

At the same time the risk is reduced by the fact that events which are the most real impose themselves the most. Here time and language conspire to influence decision in a very unique way. The time is "now." Not the "now" of a present which is the next step removed from the past, nor the "now" of a presence securely organized by its own interior meaningfulness, but the "now" of crisis, of imminence, of judgment, precipitated by a future which threatens one's present with a whole new base of organization. The language is a language of imminence because its message pertains to what is "now." Decision cannot be protracted now as judges weigh exhibits in galleries or historians sift the data in libraries. Yet the appeal of this announcement is not the rasping auctioneering of the cruder evangelisms. The language of eschatology has a benevolent immediacy, the immediacy of a Lautrec poster which by its utter transparency takes possession of the street, as one of his contemporaries described his work. Eschatological decision occurs through language which is not simply presentational but performatory. What it says to us it effects in us. One commits himself to its appeal almost as if he had not decided, as one laughs without reflecting, yet never being surprised or sorry that he has reacted so.[33] There is a luminousness in the eschatological event which blinds us only to make us see more clearly, and brings us to decisions we would not otherwise have made. But it is the sheer promise of finality in it which inspires us to throw ourselves upon this event, as the oppressed throw themselves upon the mercy of

[33] Humor is a better analogy to faith than "taste." Taste is a popular category in modern philosophy which is tempting to the theologian because it is an aspect of experience which one feels with great certainty without being able to explain why. Hans-Georg Gadamer, *Wahrheit und Methode*, Tübingen, 1960, p. 33, has explored the use of this category. The analogy from taste to faith is very misleading, however, for the very reasons adduced on its behalf. On the one hand, faith is not experienced with great certainty. There is confidence and courage but always in the dimension of risk. On the other hand, faith carries its own illumination, its own communicable interpretation, as taste does not. Thus, the category of taste encourages dogmatism, whereas faith is the antithesis of dogmatism.

their deliverers. One can understand, then, that Jean Bodin would say, "Sacred history is the most certain of all, for it is immutable."[34]

This consciousness of the reduction of our historical risk by the priority of God's meaningful activity in history is called by Christians "grace." Peter Wust, contemporary German Catholic philosopher, said in his dying moments, "I have wagered all for grace." He was right to have said he had *wagered*. Risk is always man's posture in history. In history the gravest sin is the desire for security. He was also right to have said he had wagered *all*, because in eschatological history it is a matter of all or nothing, obedience or disobedience. But he was wrong to have said he had wagered all for *grace*. Grace is the merciful aggressiveness in the eschatological event which overcomes the consciousness of risk through the sheer clarity and power by which it solicits our obedience. Georges Bernanos, the French Catholic novelist, was therefore wiser to have chosen the words of Theresa of Lisieux for the lips of his dying country priest. For in the logic of eschatological history, "*tout est grâce*"—"all is grace."

Power as Holy Spirit. Where Christians in the medieval tradition are accustomed to saying "all is grace," Protestants have learned to say "all is Holy Spirit." The decisiveness of eschatological history can be called grace because here decision occurs in man as if by gift. The power of that decisiveness, however, is what Christians call the power of the Holy Spirit.

[34] R. Gregor Smith has singled out a difference between Hamann and Kierkegaard regarding the risk of faith. For Kierkegaard there is a directness in the communication of faith which puts faith beyond the world. For Hamann, faith always includes scepticism. Smith's preference for Hamann in this instance seems to neglect the realization that Hamann thought in general historical terms; Kierkegaard in his direct discourse thought in eschatological terms. Indirectness in the appropriation of faith, therefore, was not so inescapable to Kierkegaard as to Hamann. That is why he could use the experience of humor as the analogy for how faith sweeps one off one's feet, whereas Hamann called faith humorous because it was always subject to the *giddiness* of insecurity. See R. Gregor Smith, *J. G. Hamann:* A Study in Christian Existentialism, Harper, 1960. See also Wilhelm Lüt-

Some may observe that treating the Holy Spirit in the very last section of a treatise like this is the repetition of the typical Protestant, anthropocentric error of Schleiermacher, who put the doctrine of the trinity at the end of his *Glaubenslehre* rather than at the beginning, as Karl Barth chose to. Three things should be noticed, instead. First of all, this brief treatise is not a systematic theology but at most a prolegomenon to systematic theology. That means, it is not intended to be an exposition of Christian doctrines but the suggestion of a method of thinking the Christian faith. Anything that appears anywhere, even in the last chapter, in a prolegomenon must influence the whole system which it anticipates. It is a matter of indifference, therefore, whether it appears first or last, as long as it is organic to the method of theological understanding as a whole. Second, eschatology has here been given a priority over all the other doctrines, as their key. Emil Brunner, who once said that eschatology is not the last chapter of a dogmatics but the peg on which all else hangs, has at last treated eschatology as the concluding chapter in his own *Dogmatik* (Volume III). The nineteenth-century German theologian little known in America, A. F. C. Vilmar, predicted that while nineteenth-century theology would be theology as ecclesiology, twentieth-century theology would be theology as eschatology. It is past mid-century, *Church Dogmatics* is the mode, and no one has gratified Vilmar's prophecy.

---

gert, *Die Religion des deutschen Idealismus und ihr Ende*, Vol. II, Gütersloh, third edition, 1929, pp. 1-9, a treatment of Hamann which has made Hamann's thought much more influential in the formation of contemporary German theology than Professor Smith has allowed. A similar conflict can be cited in recent times between Karl Barth and Paul Tillich. Barth's sense of humor is dictated by the overwhelming confidence by which the faith inspires the church. Tillich's sense of humor is his weapon for attacking every form of dogmatism. The form of historical understanding in general supports Tillich's version. The maturity of historical understanding as it is present in eschatology supports Barth's. Where the two dimensions of history are not distinguished in theological discourse, *rabies theologorum* results, as Karl Ludwig Schmidt described the Tillich-Barth exchange of 1923.

Finally, however, one must confess that it is impossible to do justice to the doctrine of the Holy Spirit in either a volume or a paragraph, whether first or last, for the Holy Spirit *is* the final word realizing itself historically. The Holy Spirit is eschatology operative in the whole of history. This spirit is not operative in nature, of course, for nature excludes personal relations, and the Holy Spirit is conceived preeminently in relational terms, even in the most cautious theologies of the church.[35] One might wish to say that the Holy Spirit is operative on God's behalf in history in a prevenient way, but that is nothing the church should appeal to. The church, if it understands the essentially historical character of its faith, will not bank upon the Spirit's being present anywhere prior to the church's own assumption of responsibility for interpreting the faith. The Spirit is present when the word of God in Jesus of Nazareth becomes the possibility for history's ultimately meaningful existence. When that word is declared, the Holy Spirit of God becomes effective in history.

What, however, does it mean to say "effective"? What is the connotation of "power" in the "work" of the Holy Spirit? The power of the Holy Spirit is historical power, which means the power of freedom born of light. The Holy Spirit is the eschatological spirit which Joel predicted would come in the last days. That is, the Holy Spirit illuminates by making the end present. When the church is faithful in its witness to Jesus of Nazareth, the Holy Spirit brings history to its end. The Holy Spirit, then, is the power of eschatological history. The doctrine of the Holy Spirit means that the revelation of God is imminent in an activity characterized as grace, the content of which is forgiveness and the effect of which is the creation of the church. In short, all the things that can be said of eschatological history have the Holy Spirit as their effective power.

This shift in emphasis which the Protestant Reformation intro-

[35] See my article, "The Holy Spirit and the Church," *Theology Today*, April, 1952, where the relevance of historical matters in theology was barely dawning on me.

duced is inseparable not only from the Protestant sense of faith as history but also from the notion of Christianity as history come of age. For "grace" in medieval Christianity is a quasi-substantial reality. The word of institution is present to it as its cause but not in it as its meaning. In Protestant understanding, God is believed to work not simply by but through his word. When the word of God is interpreted and God acts in such a way as to be present, it is said that the Holy Spirit has worked. The difference between grace and Holy Spirit in theological understanding is that the power of the Spirit connotes verbal power, the power of illumination. The power of grace is the power of the ineffable. That is why the Holy Spirit is an historical reality. Not because it is a force at work in history, but because where that force is at work it creates history. The doctrine of the Holy Spirit thus takes the activity of God's grace out of the realm of mythology which is history in its immaturity, by always associating God's activity with a meaningful language. Language about God which moves one to action without at the same time communicating the meaning of the act is incantation. Language about God which moves one to action, through the lucidity of its interpretation, is invocation. The power of Christian faith is in the power of the Holy Spirit, because that power is the activity in which God makes his presence meaningful through the interpretive ministry of the word in the church.

INDEX OF NAMES

INDEX OF SUBJECTS